W9-CSZ-004

The Roaring Twenties

Hal Marcovitz

Bruno Leone
Series Consultant

ReferencePoint
Press®

San Diego, CA

© 2013 ReferencePoint Press, Inc.
Printed in the United States

For more information, contact:
ReferencePoint Press, Inc.
PO Box 27779
San Diego, CA 92198
www.ReferencePointPress.com

LIBRARY OF CONGRESS CATALOGING-IN-PUBLICATION DATA

Marcovitz, Hal.
  The roaring twenties : / by Hal Marcovitz.
     p. cm.-- (Understanding American history series)
  Includes bibliographical references and index.
  ISBN-13: 978-1-60152-248-1 (hardback)
  ISBN-10: 1-60152-248-7 (hardback)
  1. United States--History--1919-1933--Juvenile literature. 2. United States--Social life and customs--1918-1945--Juvenile literature. I. Title. II. Title: Roaring twenties.
  E784.M317 2012
  973.921--dc23

                                                                          2011045415

Contents

Foreword

America's Puritan ancestors—convinced that their adopted country was blessed by God and would eventually rise to worldwide prominence—proclaimed their new homeland the shining "city upon a hill." The nation that developed since those first hopeful words were uttered has clearly achieved prominence on the world stage and it has had many shining moments but its history is not without flaws. The history of the United States is a virtual patchwork of achievements and blemishes. For example, America was originally founded as a New World haven from the tyranny and persecution prevalent in many parts of the Old World. Yet the colonial and federal governments in America took little or no action against the use of slave labor by the southern states until the 1860s, when a civil war was fought to eliminate slavery and preserve the federal union.

In the decades before and after the Civil War, the United States underwent a period of massive territorial expansion; through a combination of purchase, annexation, and war, its east–west borders stretched from the Atlantic to the Pacific Oceans. During this time, the Industrial Revolution that began in eighteenth-century Europe found its way to America, where it was responsible for considerable growth of the national economy. The United States was now proudly able to take its place in the Western Hemisphere's community of nations as a worthy economic and technological partner. Yet America also chose to join the major western European powers in a race to acquire colonial empires in Africa, Asia, and the islands of the Caribbean and South Pacific. In this scramble for empire, foreign territories were often peacefully annexed but military force was readily used when needed, as in the Philippines during the Spanish-American War of 1898.

Toward the end of the nineteenth century and concurrent with America's ambitions to acquire colonies, its vast frontier and expanding industrial base provided both land and jobs for a new and ever-growing wave of immigrants from southern and eastern Europe. Although America had always encouraged immigration, these newcomers—Italians, Greeks, and eastern European Jews, among others—were seen as different from the vast majority of earlier immigrants, most of whom were from northern and western Europe. The presence of these newcomers was treated as a matter of growing concern, which in time evolved into intense opposition. Congress boldly and with calculated prejudice set out to create a barrier to curtail the influx of unwanted nationalities and ethnic groups to America's shores. The outcome was the National Origins Act, passed in 1924. That law severely reduced immigration to the United States from southern and eastern Europe. Ironically, while this was happening, the Statue of Liberty stood in New York Harbor as a visible and symbolic beacon lighting the way for people of *all* nationalities and ethnicities seeking sanctuary in America.

Unquestionably, the history of the United States has not always mirrored that radiant beacon touted by the early settlers. As often happens, reality and dreams tend to move in divergent directions. However, the story of America also reveals a people who have frequently extended a helping hand to a weary world and who have displayed a ready willingness—supported by a flexible federal constitution—to take deliberate and effective steps to correct injustices, past and present. America's private and public philanthropy directed toward other countries during times of natural disasters (such as the contributions of financial and human resources to assist Haiti following the January 2010, earthquake) and the legal right to adopt amendments to the US Constitution (including the Thirteenth Amendment freeing the slaves and the Nineteenth Amendment granting women the right to vote) are examples of the nation's generosity and willingness to acknowledge and reverse wrongs.

With objectivity and candor, the titles selected for the Understanding American History series portray the many sides of America, depicting both its shining moments and its darker hours. The series strives to help readers achieve a wider understanding and appreciation of the American experience and to encourage further investigation into America's evolving character and founding principles.

Important Events of the Roaring Twenties

1920
On January 17, the Eighteenth Amendment to the US Constitution becomes law, prohibiting the sale and consumption of alcoholic beverages.

1918
On November 11 the armistice ends World War I. The League of Nations is soon established to settle international disputes before they erupt in warfare, but the United States refuses to join.

1922
The American Appliance Company develops a plug-in electric radio.

1870 **1920** **1922**

1873
The Woman's Christian Temperance Union forms in Fredonia, New York. The union works toward prohibition of alcoholic beverages and maintains pressure on political leaders during the 1920s to keep the law intact.

1915
William Simmons reestablishes the Ku Klux Klan, the racist organization that would be instrumental in denying civil rights to African Americans throughout the 1920s.

1923
New York gangster Owney Madden opens the Cotton Club in New York, featuring the hottest performers in jazz. Madden restricts entry to whites only, while blacks work as entertainers or in menial jobs.

1919
On June 2 nine bombs set by anarchists explode around Washington, DC; miraculously, there are no injuries. The incident sets off the Palmer raids, in which some 10,000 suspected Communists are rounded up and deported.

1921
Margaret Sanger establishes the American Birth Control League; among the founding members are physicians as well as other advocates for women's health.

1924
Movie stuntman Alvin "Shipwreck" Kelly inaugurates the national phenomenon of flagpole sitting when he sits on a perch atop a flagpole for more than 13 hours; years later he will set the record for remaining atop a flagpole for seven weeks.

1928
Herbert Hoover is elected president; like his two predecessors, Hoover pledges little government intervention in people's lives.

1926
Harlem Renaissance poet Langston Hughes publishes his first book of poetry, *The Weary Blues*, helping spark the civil rights movement.

1932
Franklin D. Roosevelt is elected in a landslide, promising Americans a New Deal, a series of social programs that help rebuild the American economy.

| 1924 | 1926 | 1928 | 1930 | 1932 |

1929
On October 24—Black Thursday—the stock market drops 9 percent in value; another 13 percent drop is recorded five days later. The stock market crash would continue through 1932, propelling the country into the Great Depression.

1925
John T. Scopes goes on trial for breaking a Tennessee law that prohibits the teaching of evolution. Scopes is convicted and fined $100, but the Tennessee Supreme Court overturns the conviction two years later.

1933
Congress and the state legislatures ratify the Twenty-First Amendment to the US Constitution, repealing Prohibition.

1927
Aviator Charles Lindbergh arrives in Paris, France, on the evening of May 21, becoming the first pilot to fly nonstop across the Atlantic Ocean.

The Defining Characteristics of the Roaring Twenties

The crowd had been gathering for hours at the First Congregational Church in Norfolk, Virginia, the tabernacle of the Reverend Billy Sunday. It was the evening of January 16, 1920. In just a few hours, the Eighteenth Amendment of the US Constitution—also known as Prohibition—would take effect, outlawing the sale and consumption of alcoholic beverages. Hundreds of "drys," as supporters of Prohibition were known, held a rally at Sunday's church to celebrate victory in their long campaign to outlaw beer, wine, and liquor.

A nationally known evangelist, Sunday had been preaching against the evils of alcohol for years. "The man who votes for the saloon is pulling the same rope with the devil, whether he knows it or not,"[1] Sunday once declared. Another nationally known figure who attended the rally was William Jennings Bryan. Three times an unsuccessful candidate for president, Bryan had campaigned for adoption of the Eighteenth Amendment with as much zeal as he had campaigned for the White House. At the stroke of midnight, as the Eighteenth Amendment became law, Bryan faced the crowd and declared "the nation would be saloonless forever."[2]

Meanwhile, hundreds of miles away, six masked men jumped out of a truck at a railroad switching yard in Chicago, Illinois. Brandishing guns, they tied up a night watchman, then broke into railroad freight cars, stealing $100,000 worth of whiskey that had been reserved for medicinal use. (A provision in the new law permitted small quantities of liquor to be dispensed by physicians, evidently for its painkilling properties.) These men had no intentions of selling the liquor to doctors—they planned to sell it to the proprietors of illegal saloons known as speakeasies.

A Time of Excitement and Risk

The incident in Chicago illustrates that as Bryan, Sunday, and other drys heralded the arrival of Prohibition, others with far more devious motives were also celebrating. For the nation's gangsters, it would be

After taking an ax to a barrel of beer, a prohibitionist dumps the beer into the street—a scene that was repeated again and again throughout the 1920s. The ban on the sale and consumption of alcoholic beverages, known as Prohibition, was one of the defining events of the period.

the beginning of a lawless period, a time of excitement and risk, when ordinary people would defy an unpopular law. The 1920s had arrived with a roar—hence, the nickname for the decade: the Roaring Twenties. It would be a time of tremendous change as America broke with the stodgy ways of the past. Writing about the dawn of the decade, novelist F. Scott Fitzgerald said, "There seemed to be little doubt about what was going to happen—America was going on the greatest, gaudiest spree in history and there was going to be plenty to tell about it. The whole golden boom was in the air—its splendid generosities, its outrageous corruptions and the tortuous death struggle of the old America."[3]

The Roaring Twenties were about much more than Prohibition and those who defied it. The technical achievements of the decade helped tie the nation together as radios and automobiles became available to ordinary people. Great advances were also made in cinema and aviation. In the arts some of America's greatest writers, artists, musicians, and other performers first gained prominence in the 1920s.

Fashion reflected the spirit of the times as many women discarded the prim, ankle-length styles of the previous decade for higher hemlines as well as bobbed hairstyles and showy costume jewelry. The decade also gave birth to its own music. It was called jazz, and it could be bouncy and bright or soulful and sweet. Meanwhile, baseball players found themselves achieving the status of national celebrities as they revolutionized their sport.

Era of Radical Change

But the Roaring Twenties were more than just a decade-long party. In Russia the Bolshevik movement had ousted a long-despised monarchy. Americans found much to fear in this new movement that was based on the principles of communism—state ownership of agriculture and

A women's fashion magazine, circa 1920, promotes the latest spring and summer styles. During the 1920s, many women abandoned the somber attire of past generations in favor of bright colors, sleek fabrics, and playful styles.

industry. To root out Communists, American political leaders resorted to tactics that often violated the constitutional rights of those suspected of anarchy and plotting to overthrow the US government. New immigrants from Europe found themselves under suspicion, and many were deported on scant evidence.

Meanwhile, the first voices in the civil rights movement were making themselves heard, but they were often met with the iron fist of the racist and violent Ku Klux Klan, which found widespread popularity among rural whites who refused to accept African Americans as equals. While Americans struggled with these issues at home, fascist movements in Germany, Italy, Japan, and other countries were growing in influence and would, over the next 20 years, hatch schemes for world domination that would draw them into armed conflict with America and other nations.

Still, at the dawn of the Roaring Twenties, most people looked forward to an era of prosperity and radical change. Says author and historian Ronald Allen Goldberg:

> The decade of the 1920s was a time of remarkable cultural changes in American society. This was a period of amazing vitality, social invention and change, and the formative years of modern America. Because it became an urban nation for the first time simultaneously with a technical revolution that led to mass production and mass consumption, the United States saw a hastened breakdown of old habits and patterns of thought and the start of drastic changes in American lifestyle.[4]

Chapter 1

What Conditions Led to the Roaring Twenties?

The Roaring Twenties arrived on the heels of one of the most horrific episodes in the history of world civilization. Known at the time as the Great War, and today as World War I, the conflict cost nearly 14 million lives worldwide. America did not join the conflict until the last year of the war. Even so, more than 100,000 American soldiers were killed in action, and another 200,000 were wounded by the time of the declaration of the armistice on November 11, 1918.

In Europe, where most of the fighting occurred, long-established monarchies fell, replaced by fledgling and unsteady democracies. Indeed, Russia, which had commenced the war as an enemy of Germany and its allies, fell victim to revolution even before the war had ended. After the war, Germany, Austria, Hungary, Turkey, and other countries that fought on the losing side were plagued by political turmoil and economic woes as they attempted to rebuild their societies and fashion new governments. Even some of the victors, including France and Italy, would find difficulties ahead as their governments fell into hostile factions, causing stalemate and preventing them from improving the lives of their people.

America emerged from the Great War as a world power. President Woodrow Wilson believed the end of the conflict represented an opportunity for the forces of democracy to set the tone for international politics. He proposed establishment of the League of Nations, where international disputes would be settled.

But the league was never effective, mostly because the United States never joined—Wilson was unable to convince a US Senate dominated by isolationists to approve membership. These influential senators—watching the turmoil that engulfed the European countries—believed America should have no role in the affairs of other nations. "The United States is the world's best hope but . . . if you tangle her in the intrigues of Europe, you will destroy her power for good and endanger her very existence,"[5] insisted Senator Henry Cabot Lodge, a staunch opponent of the league.

Rise of the Temperance Movement

All of this political wrangling dominated the headlines in the months following the armistice and well into 1919 and the presidential campaign of 1920. And so, when presidential candidate Warren G. Harding pledged a "return to normalcy"[6]—in other words, a return to the peaceful way of life Americans had known before the war—many Americans responded to his message and sent the Ohio senator to the White House. Harding promised a laissez-faire policy toward business, meaning the government would enact few regulations on American industries, giving them a chance to grow. Indeed, Harding promised that during his administration the government would stay out of everyone's lives. Said Harding, "In the great fulfillment we must have a citizenship less concerned about what the government can do for it and more anxious about what it can do for the nation."[7]

However, the one corner of American life in which the government would definitely intrude was the drinking habits of its citizens. The Eighteenth Amendment and the enforcement arm of the new law—the Volstead Act—went into effect as the 1920s got under way. Prohibition was the result of a decades-long campaign by an anti-alcohol movement that had blossomed after the Civil War. The movement's most vocal advocates were members of the Woman's Christian Temperance Union (WCTU), which first organized in 1873 in Fredonia, New York. Soon chapters had formed in many cities and towns. By the end of the nineteenth century, the WCTU was one of the most politically powerful organizations in the country.

The Volstead and Jones Acts

To enforce the Eighteenth Amendment to the US Constitution, Congress passed the National Prohibition Act in October 1919. The act is more familiarly known as the Volstead Act because it is named after its author, Representative Andrew Volstead of Minnesota. The law defined intoxicating liquors as any beverage with an alcoholic content of at least 0.5 percent. The Volstead Act also set penalties for violators—two years in prison and fines of $1,000 for first-time offenders.

Statistics show those penalties hardly dissuaded the bootleggers—some of whom were raking in millions of dollars—from manufacturing and selling illegal alcoholic beverages. By 1929 more than 340,000 people had been convicted of violations of the Volstead Act. In 1929 Congress decided a tougher law was needed to ensure compliance with the Eighteenth Amendment. That year a new measure, the Jones Act, was adopted. Authored by Senator Wesley L. Jones of Washington State, the act increased the jail term to five years and the fine to $10,000. The act also doubled the fine for repeat offenders. Moreover, the Jones Act included a provision that enabled police to padlock the doors of speakeasies whose owners were convicted of selling alcoholic beverages.

Members of the WCTU believed alcohol abuse was at the root of most of the ills that afflicted Americans. They believed that men who imbibed were poor husbands, unable to hold jobs and provide for their families. They suggested that alcohol consumption led men to abuse their wives and children and walk out on their families. Frances Willard, who served as WCTU president from 1879 to 1898, suggested that men learned to drink while still boys, picking up lifelong habits that affect their intelligence. "Boys are baited with beer and enticed into saloons by music, games and evil company,"[8] she said.

To dramatize their mission, members of the WCTU as well as other activists would often march to saloons and demand they be closed down. Since saloons often served as the meeting places for political parties, the men enjoying their drinks inside found themselves facing the angry wives of voters. (This was the era before women were granted the right to vote.) Pressured by hordes of angry constituents, many of these politicians could not help but feel pressure to act.

Carry Nation Swings Her Ax

While the women of the WCTU staged protests at the saloon doors, other activists took their opposition to alcohol a step further. The ax-wielding Carry Nation would often lead groups of angry temperance activists right into the saloons. Swinging her ax, Nation attacked the bars, barstools, beer barrels, bottles of liquor, and anything else she could find, until bartenders, police officers or customers managed to wrestle the ax out of her hands.

A typical encounter occurred at a saloon in a Wichita, Kansas, hotel. Storming into the saloon, Nation asked the bartender, "Young man, what are you doing in this hellhole?"

"I'm sorry, madam," replied the bartender, "but we do not serve ladies."

"Serve me?" she asked. "Do you think I'd drink your hellish poison?"

Nation told the bartender to close the saloon and left. The next day she returned with a club in hand and started smashing bottles and furniture. When a hotel security officer finally intervened, he found her pounding a spittoon with her club. "Madam," he said, "I must arrest you for defacing property."

"Defacing?" she replied. "I am destroying!"[9] From 1900 to 1910 Nation was arrested more than 30 times, mostly on charges of damaging private property.

By 1917 the temperance movement had gained widespread support; that year a resolution approving the Eighteenth Amendment was passed by both houses of Congress. The amendment then went to the states for ratification. On January 16, 1919, the Nebraska legislature ratified the amendment, giving the "drys" the two-thirds majority of the states that was required to amend the constitution.

Bathtub Gin

Americans largely ignored the new law that made it illegal to drink alcoholic beverages. Prohibition-era drinkers could be found everywhere in America—in big cities and small towns as well as in rural farming communities. During the 1920s Americans became familiar with the term *bathtub gin*—gin distilled by mixing grain alcohol with the berries from juniper trees. Bathtub gin earned its name because people made it themselves in their bathrooms. Historians James Kirby Martin and Mark Edward Lender explain the process: "The most common recipe was simple: Mix the alcohol with 30 to 50 percent water, then add a few drops of glycerine and juniper juice to simulate the flavor of gin. The concoction went into bottles or jugs too tall to fill with water from a sink tap, but they fit under bathtub taps, whence the term 'bathtub gin.'"[10]

Other amateur distillers found ways to make scotch whiskey, bourbon, rye, and other spirits. Often the ingredients included industrial-strength alcohol and other chemicals that were otherwise regarded as harmful if consumed. But the home-based distillers used plenty of water to cut the effectiveness of these hazardous substances; certainly, though, many drinkers risked sickness and even death whenever they consumed these homemade concoctions.

Ethnic Gangs

People who made liquor in their bathrooms soon discovered a thriving marketplace for their handiwork. Local gangs were willing to buy as much liquor as people could make. Indeed, by the dawn of the 1920s many gangs had already established themselves in the nation's biggest cities. Prior to the Prohibition era, these gangs ran illegal gambling enterprises. They also specialized in narcotics, extortion, stealing cargo from trucks, and all manner of other illegal activities. When the government outlawed the sale and consumption of alcoholic beverages, it was a relatively simple matter for the gangs to step in and take over the illegal trade in beer and liquor.

The gangs were largely ethnically based: There were Irish gangs, Italian gangs, and Jewish gangs. They recruited their members from the waves of immigrants who arrived in the country in the late 1800s and early 1900s. At the time there were few restraints on immigration

Many immigrants who arrived in the United States at the dawn of the 1920s lived in crowded tenement apartments in neighborhoods where jobs were scarce and poverty commonplace. The neighborhood around New York City's busy Orchard Street (pictured here around 1923) was one such community.

to America—virtually anyone who could afford the price of passage on a steamship could find a new home there. Indeed, by 1920 nearly 14 million Americans—about 13 percent of the US population—had been born in another country.

Many of those new citizens emigrated from impoverished conditions in European countries. One emigrant, Salvatore Lucania, left the tiny Italian village of Lercara Friddi in 1906 with his family at the age of nine. The Lucanias settled in New York City. Years later Lucania returned to Lercara Friddi to find conditions had not changed. He wrote, "There was the same stink of the sulfur mines outside our village where my father used to work. There was the same kind of gray dust coverin' everythin', and I remembered how it used to get so deep into our clothes that our mothers couldn't wash it out. And there was the same smell. It was the smell of no money, the smell of bein' hungry all the time."[11]

Rum Rows

Immigrants like Lucania may have fled such poverty with dreams of finding riches in America, but for most immigrants those dreams would prove elusive. After arriving in their new homeland, most immigrants found themselves living in poverty, crammed into tiny tenement apartments in New York, Chicago, and other overcrowded cities. Those lucky enough to find work were forced to scrape by on low wages, working long hours in dank factories and sweatshops or as manual laborers. But many immigrants could not find jobs at all and, out of desperation, turned to crime.

Lucania was one of those immigrants. To escape the poverty of his Lower East Side neighborhood in New York, Lucania formed his own gang of street toughs. Lucania's gang survived turf wars and grew in power, and by the dawn of the 1920s it had become one of the fiercest gangs operating in New York. As for Lucania, he changed his name to Charlie "Lucky" Luciano. For most of the Roaring Twenties, the Luciano mob reigned over the illegal alcohol trade in New York.

As Luciano and other mobsters gained power, it soon became evident to them that home-based operations producing a few bottles of

The Urbanization of America

As the 1920s arrived, America had largely transformed itself from a rural, agrarian society to an urban society in which most people lived in cities. Immigrants arriving in America in the late 1800s and early 1900s settled in the cities. Moreover, as the industrial revolution swept through the country, many native-born Americans left their farms for better-paying jobs in factories, which were usually located in port cities like New York, Philadelphia, and Boston. Factories in port cities could make use of ships to receive raw materials and transport finished products to their markets.

In the 50 years from 1870 to 1920, the number of Americans living in cities grew from 10 million to 54 million. At the dawn of the 1920s, for the first time in American history, there were more Americans living in cities than on farms or in small towns. Says University of Alabama history professor Raymond A. Mohl, "The face of urban America was reshaped and restructured by technology, transportation, economic development, demographic shifts and the rise of corporations. . . . The large American industrial city—for the most part ugly, congested, noisy, smelly, smoky, unhealthy, and ill-governed—emerged during this period."

Raymond A. Mohl, ed., *The Making of Urban America.* Lanham, MD: SR, 2006, p. 93.

bathtub gin a week could not supply enough liquor to quench the thirst of Americans. Luciano and the other mobsters built their own illegal distilleries and breweries. They also set up smuggling operations to transport liquor into the United States across the Canadian border or ship it past US Coast Guard vessels that patrolled coastal waters. Many of these boats were loaded with thousands of cases of liquor obtained in European port cities or cargoes of rum from the islands of the Caribbean.

Typically, these ships would drop anchor outside the 3-mile (4.8km) limit that marked the boundary of Coast Guard jurisdiction. The line of these ships anchored and waiting to offload their illegal cargoes was known as a rum row. Under the cover of darkness, tiny speedboats made their way to a rum row, loaded up with liquor, then sped back to shore, avoiding the Coast Guard patrols as well as rival gangs intent on hijacking their cargoes. Recalled Luciano, "That three miles of ocean was loaded with sharks—federal men, hijackers with speedboats. A guy could easily get killed at that time for a case of scotch. And, of course, sometimes we'd lose a truck or even a whole shipment to the Feds or to some hijackers, and we'd have to write it off."[12]

Women in the Workforce

Most drinkers did not care whether their liquor was made in a bath-tub or imported under the cover of darkness by sleek speedboats dodg-ing Coast Guard patrols. There were other issues that dominated their lives, particularly the lives of women. As the 1920s got under way, women found themselves with a degree of political power that they had been denied since the birth of the republic. On August 18, 1920, the Nineteenth Amendment to the US Constitution was ratified, granting women the right to vote. Within a short time, 9.5 million women were added to the voter registration rolls of the United States.

Moreover, as America entered the twentieth century, many women entered the American workforce as they saw their roles in society evolv-ing into more than just those of wives and mothers. In 1900, women made up 18 percent of the American workforce; by 1920 that number had grown to 21 percent, and by the end of the 1920s nearly a quarter of American workers were women.

US Labor Department studies conducted during the 1920s found that women worked mostly in factories, offices, and retail stores. Al-though women made up a growing percentage of the American work-force, their pay did not equal salaries earned by male workers. The

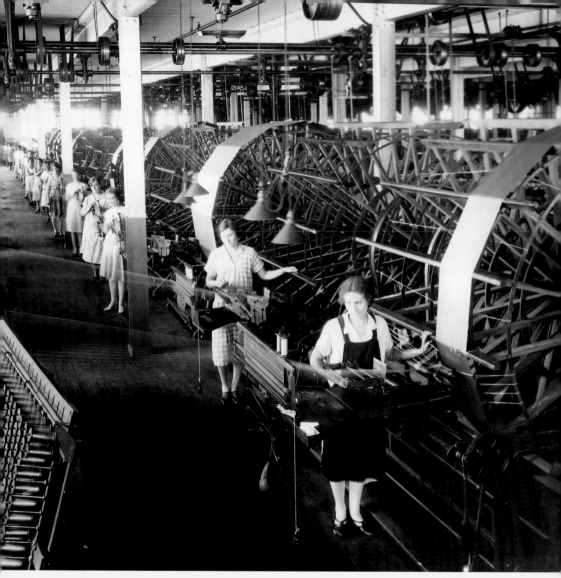

Traditional roles began changing in the United States in the early 1900s as growing numbers of women entered the workforce. Many women found jobs in factories, such as the silk factory pictured here, circa 1920.

National Industry Conference Board, a private organization of the era that studied trends in the American workplace, found that in 1927 the average weekly wage for male workers was $29.35, while the average wage for women was $17.36.

The main reason for the inequality in pay was the reluctance of a male-dominated society to accept working women on the same plane as working men. In medicine, for example, men were the doctors and women worked as nurses. Law schools placed quotas on their female enrollments, ensuring that the legal profession would be made up mostly of men. On the other hand, female schoolteachers outnumbered male schoolteachers—but few women were able to achieve the higher-paying jobs as principals and other administrators. Those jobs generally went to men.

Sexual Liberation

If the 1920s marked the first era of women's liberation in America, the decade also marked the beginning of sexual liberation as well. A decade before, the ideas of such intellectuals as Sigmund Freud began to gain traction among women. In 1909 the Austrian psychoanalyst gave a series of lectures at Clark University in Worcester, Massachusetts, in which he suggested that women had the right to pursue sexual pleasure.

Freud's ideas ran counter to the turn-of-the-century mindset of many Americans who felt that proper women should remain chaste until their wedding nights whereas unmarried men should have the freedom to enjoy carnal relations with multiple partners. Sitting in the audience during one of Freud's Clark University lectures, feminist leader Emma Goldman found herself stunned by his message. Said Goldman:

> His simplicity and earnestness and the brilliance of his mind combined to give one the feeling of being led out of a dark cellar into broad daylight. For the first time I grasped the full significance of sex repression and its effect on human thought and action. He helped me to understand myself, my own needs; and I also realized that only people of depraved minds could impugn the motives or find "impure" so great and fine a personality as Freud.[13]

To be truly sexually liberated, though, women would need to practice contraception, which prior to the 1920s was not widely available to most women. Margaret Sanger discovered that women were largely denied access to contraceptives soon after she enrolled in nursing school at the age of 17. For the most part, she found, contraceptives such as diaphragms and spermicidal jellies were expensive and generally only available to wealthy women.

Moreover, Sanger discovered that this lack of contraception had ill effects on poor women and other women of modest means. Sanger found many of these women suffered ill health, which she blamed on the demands on their bodies caused by multiple pregnancies and child-births. In fact, she blamed the early death of her mother, at the age of 50, on her father's insistence on a large family—Sanger was one of 11 children. She said:

> So great was the ignorance of women and girls concerning their own bodies that I decided to specialize in women's diseases and took up gynecological and obstetrical nursing. A few years of this work brought me to the shocking discovery—the knowl-edge of the ways of controlling birth were accessible to the women of wealth while the working women were deliberately kept in ignorance of this knowledge.[14]

Sanger became a zealous advocate for birth control and in 1916 helped establish the nation's first birth control clinic in New York City. On opening day, 150 women stood in line to receive contraceptives dis-persed by the clinic. In 1921 she established the American Birth Con-trol League, whose members included physicians and other advocates for women's health. Eventually, the league was merged into another group that still exists today, the Planned Parenthood Federation of America.

Lawless Era

At the dawn of the 1920s, it was clear that the decade would be un-like any other in American history. It would be a decade of change as people moved beyond the long-established ways of the past. American women demanded the same employment opportunities as men; they also demanded the right to vote as well as the right to decide whether to have children.

Other changes in American society were less welcome. Members of Congress refused to approve America's entry into the League of Nations, insisting that the United States remain isolated from the problems brewing in postwar Europe. Certainly, many Americans did not embrace Prohibition. In the years to come, many ordinary people who would never think of breaking the law by stealing or doing harm to a neighbor would be more than willing to buy and consume illegal liquor and beer. Americans' desire to break an unpopular law would help gangsters like Lucky Luciano grow rich and powerful while also providing the Roaring Twenties with its reputation as an edgy, exciting, and lawless era.

Chapter 2

The Jazz Age

On Saint Valentine's Day in 1929, a large black sedan entered a garage on North Clark Street in Chicago. This particular garage was well known in the underworld as the North Side Gang's storehouse for bootleg beer and liquor. The gang was headed by mobster George "Bugs" Moran. For years Moran's gang had been fighting a turf war over control of the illegal alcohol business with a rival gang headed by mobster Alphonse "Al" Capone.

The sedan came to a stop inside the garage. Five men got out: Three wore the uniform of the Chicago police; two were dressed in street clothes and appeared to be detectives. Moments later witnesses outside the garage heard the loud clatter of gunshots. Suddenly, the black sedan left the garage and sped off.

Curious bystanders crept into the garage. They found the bodies of six dead men; a seventh victim was still alive but would soon succumb to his gunshot wounds as well. All were members of the Moran gang. They had been lined up against a wall and executed by the gunmen who arrived in the black sedan.

Moran escaped the slaughter, arriving at the garage just as the black sedan pulled in. Seeing the uniformed "police officers" in the car, he suspected a raid by the Chicago police and fled the scene. When he returned and saw the carnage for himself, he said, "Only Capone kills like that."[15]

The gunmen were, in fact, not members of the Chicago police but instead thugs employed in the service of Capone. The newspapers soon dubbed the shooting the Saint Valentine's Day Massacre. Details of the shooting horrified readers, but in reality the decade of the 1920s was marked by similar acts of violence as competing mobs fought over the lucrative bootleg alcohol business.

Although alcoholic beverages were now banned by law, the Eighteenth Amendment and the Volstead Act were largely ignored by the public. Much of the bootleg alcohol was sold in illegal nightclubs known as speakeasies. Some of these establishments operated behind closed doors under a veil of secrecy, but others operated in the open, making no attempt to hide what was going on inside. These clubs were largely owned by wealthy and powerful mobsters who could bribe the police and political leaders to allow them to remain in business.

The Cotton Club

Among the most prominent of these establishments was the Cotton Club in the Harlem neighborhood of New York City. In the 1920s Harlem was populated mostly by African Americans—as it is today. In 1921 ex-heavyweight boxing champion Jack Johnson opened a nightclub in Harlem he named Café de Luxe (in English, Café of Luxury.)

The ex-champ lost money on the club, and in 1922 he was forced to sell it to mobster Owney Madden. In 1923 Madden reopened the nightspot as the Cotton Club. He made sure it would be the hottest place in town, featuring the top singers, dancers, and musicians of the era.

Inside, the scene was incandescent. Tuxedoed men accompanied women wearing the latest fashions—short skirts, bobbed haircuts, and gaudy jewelry. These women smoked cigarettes, drank liquor, drove cars, and often stayed out all night—leaving behind the previous decade's archaic image of the wife and mother whose prime responsibility was to husband, home, and family. These women were known as "flappers." They enjoyed doing the popular dances of the era, moving to the quick rhythms of such dances as the Charleston, Varsity Drag, Black Bottom, Shimmy, and Lindy Hop.

On the Cotton Club stage, the performers included some of the top African American singers and musicians of an era that would soon be known as the Jazz Age. Among these performers were Duke Ellington, Cab Calloway, Ethel Waters, Louis Armstrong, Lena Horne, Bill Robinson, and Billy Eckstine. As pianist Earl "Fatha" Hines recalled, in

Patrons of popular nightspots such as Harlem's Cotton Club wore the latest fashions of the time. Men in tuxedos accompanied women in flapper styles that included short dresses, feather boas, and bobbed haircuts (as seen in this 1920s era photograph).

reference to the Jazz Age, "It all started in the Roaring Twenties, when short skirts, bobbed hair and bootleg whiskey made nightclubs an important phase of American life."[16]

These performers helped make jazz a widely popular form of American music. In fact, jazz can trace its roots as far back as the 1840s to the folk music of African Americans, most of them slaves. It was in these songs that the beats, harmonies and melodies of what became modern jazz first surfaced. Many historians of music suggest that the African American musicians in 1900s New Orleans crafted these elements into the jazz sound—brassy melodies, bluesy lyrics, and lots of improvisation. Says jazz historian Leonard Feather, "Written music was rarely needed."[17]

Jazz crossed color lines, appealing to white audiences. Soon white performers such as Bix Beiderbecke, Paul Whiteman, and Jack Teagarden became major jazz artists of the 1920s.

Big Crowds on Broadway

The popularity of jazz led to the emergence of dance as a national phenomenon. Speakeasies like the Cotton Club always featured chorus lines made up of leggy dancers wearing costumes with sequins and feathers. Extravagant musicals premiered on the Broadway stage, all featuring elaborately choreographed dance performances. The public's appetite for Broadway musicals seemed insatiable—by the end the 1920s, 66 theaters had opened either on or near Broadway in New York. In a typical year during the 1920s, 225 new shows opened in Broadway theaters. Many closed soon after their premieres, but many would run for hundreds of performances. The theaters also featured dramas as well as comedies, but musicals were always the most popular shows, bringing in the biggest crowds.

One of the big Broadway hits of the era was the musical comedy *Sally*, which was staged by impresario Florenz Ziegfeld. The musical featured tap dancer Marilyn Miller and ran for 570 performances from 1920 through 1924. Miller also starred in another 1920s hit musical— *Sunny*, the first play to feature the collaboration of composer Jerome Kern and lyricist Oscar Hammerstein II. *Sunny* premiered in 1925 and ran for 517 performances. As for Kern and Hammerstein, their partnership would produce numerous shows, including the Broadway hit *Show Boat*—regarded by many critics as the greatest musical ever produced.

Dancer Fred Astaire—who would go on to become one of the biggest movie stars of the twentieth century—made his Broadway debut in 1917. By the 1920s he was one of Broadway's top performers. He starred in the 1924 musical *Lady Be Good!*, with music and lyrics by George and Ira Gershwin, brothers who would collaborate on many hit Broadway and movie musicals.

Dance Marathons

As much as the public may have loved musical theater and dance, the price of a Broadway ticket was usually well beyond the means of most people. During the 1920s a ticket to a Broadway show typically cost $3.50—a small amount by today's standards, but in the 1920s, $3.50 could often amount to a day's pay.

High ticket prices meant that only the well-to-do could regularly attend Broadway shows. Most other people had to find other venues to enjoy music and dance. Soon impresarios started staging dance marathons—contests in which couples danced for hours, and often days or weeks, at a time. For an admission price of a mere 25 cents, a spectator could watch the competition and listen to the dance band for as long as he or she desired.

As for the contestants, they vied for cash prizes in these competitions, often known as "bunion derbies" and "corn and callus carnivals." Dancers were expected to stay on their feet for days or weeks at a time, although they were given brief breaks to rest several times a day. Dance

Jazz age nightclubs boasted the top musicians of the time, including African American performers such as Louis Armstrong (pictured here playing his trumpet in the mid-twentieth century). These performers helped make jazz one of the most widely popular forms of American music.

marathons typically drew dozens of contestants and hundreds of spectators, but many people found them in poor taste and even hazardous to the health of the dancers. In 1928 a Seattle, Washington, woman attempted suicide after making it through a dance marathon for 19 days—only to finish in fifth place. Some cities adopted local ordinances outlawing the marathons. A reporter for the *New York World* described the typical marathon for the paper's readers:

> The dingy hall, littered with worn slippers, cigarette stubs, newspapers and soup cans; reeking with the mingled odors of stale coffee, tobacco smoke, cold broth, chewing gum and smelling salts, was the scene of one of the most drab and grueling endurance contests ever witnessed. There is nothing inspiring in seeing an extremely tired pretty girl in a worn bathrobe, dingy white stockings in . . . felt slippers, her eyes half shut, her arms hung around her partner's shoulders, drag aching feet that seemed glued to the floor in one short, agonizing step after another.[18]

The public's thirst for bizarre forms of entertainment went beyond dance marathons. Some daredevils staged much different types of marathons: During the 1920s, the spectacle of flagpole sitting grew in popularity. The nation's top performer was movie stuntman Alvin "Shipwreck" Kelly, who first ascended to a perch atop a flagpole in Los Angeles, California, in 1924 and remained there for 13 hours and 13 minutes. Others duplicated Kelly's stunt, and soon a national competition was under way. Kelly would not be outdone—whenever a competitor set a new record, he vowed to retrieve the crown. Finally, in 1929, Kelly spent 49 days atop a flagpole in Atlantic City, New Jersey, while crowds totaling 10,000 or more gathered below each day to witness the champion set a record for flagpole sitting that would never be broken.

Catering to the Wealthy

Of course, a nightclub as classy as the Cotton Club would never stage a dance marathon. The Cotton Club catered to the wealthy and prominent people of New York. The club could hold as many as 700 patrons, who arrived each night to drink bootleg liquor, listen to the jazz performers, and watch the lively stage shows featuring leggy chorus girls.

Madden made no attempt to hide what was going on at the Cotton Club. Alcoholic beverages were sold openly and with the full knowledge of the police and local politicians, whom he bribed to look the other way. Indeed, chances were that on any given night, New York City mayor James J. "Beau James" Walker could be found entertaining his friends and cronies at a Cotton Club table. Walker loved the New York nightlife and maintained affairs with chorus girls at a number of speakeasies.

Beau James

Elected mayor of New York City in 1925, James J. Walker soon made it clear that he had no intention of enforcing the laws against alcoholic beverages. Walker enjoyed the nightlife; he could often be seen at the Cotton Club and other posh speakeasies with beautiful actress Betty Compton on his arm.

Known as "Beau James" or "Gentleman Jimmy," Walker turned a blind eye as the police and political leaders took bribes to ensure the speakeasies stayed open. By the late 1920s it was estimated that some 30,000 speakeasies were operating in New York.

Walker was always ready to accept bribes. In one infamous case, a contractor paid a bribe of nearly $250,000 to the mayor to secure the contract for installing tiles in the New York subway stations. Despite the air of corruption that hung over his administration, Walker remained popular with the voters and won reelection in 1929.

His corrupt ways continued, but in 1932, with investigators closing in, he abruptly resigned and fled to Europe to avoid prosecution. While living in Europe, he married Compton. As the threat of prosecution receded, he returned to New York in 1935, taking a job with a record company. Walker died in 1946 of a brain hemorrhage at the age of 65.

Each night, expensive cars such as Duesenbergs, Packards, and Stutzes stopped in front of the club on Harlem's Lenox Avenue, disgorging such fun seekers as heiresses Emily Vanderbilt and Edwina Mountbatten, actress Ann Pennington, and investor Sailing Baruch. These patrons may have been at the top of New York society, but they also found it thrilling to share a table with the likes of Madden and other tough guys. Recalled Hines:

> It was an open secret that the chief investor in the Cotton Club was the fabulous and feared Owney Madden. . . . Allied with Madden in direct ownership of the Cotton Club was George "Frenchy" DeMange, another colorful character in the Manhattan underworld that had its tentacles running into City Hall. . . .
>
> Both Madden and Frenchy were seen often at the Cotton Club surrounded by beautiful high-powered women. They spent on a fabulous scale and tipped on a grand manner. Frenchy was a regular partner in card games with Duke Ellington. He was personally known to practically all the big name entertainers who ever worked at the club—people like Cab Calloway, Ethel Waters, Bill Robinson and all the world-famous beauties in the chorus.[19]

The Cotton Club was not the only speakeasy in town—it was not unusual for thousands of speakeasies to be operating in the big cities of America. The bootleg liquor trade was a business that was run by mobsters who were not opposed to using strong-arm tactics. When Calloway was offered more money to appear at the Plantation Club, just a few blocks up Lenox Avenue, Madden sent a gang of thugs to vandalize the rival showroom. Calloway elected to stay at the Cotton Club.

The Rise of Capone

Madden was only one of the top mobsters, also known as racketeers, in 1920s New York. Others were Lucky Luciano, who was raking in millions as a bootlegger while also running gambling and prostitution

Dance marathons, sometimes lasting for weeks at a time, attracted couples hoping to win cash prizes. One such event, at New York's Coney Island in 1928, attracted 40 couples (pictured).

rackets; gambler Arnold Rothstein, who is alleged to have fixed the 1919 World Series; Arthur Flegenheimer, also known as Dutch Schultz, a known killer with his hands in the illegal liquor and gambling rackets; Vincent "Mad Dog" Coll, a notorious killer and one of Flegenheimer's enforcers; and bootlegger Jack "Legs" Diamond, who was so wealthy that he was known to offer Cotton Club musicians tips of $1,000 for playing his favorite songs. After Ellington honored Diamond's request to play the song *St. Louis Blues*, Diamond handed the pianist a rolled-up $1,000 bill and told him to buy himself a cigar. Replied Ellington, "I don't know where I could buy a cigar that expensive."[20] Diamond laughed—and then tipped Ellington another $1,000.

Chicago was also home to many racketeers, but in Chicago there was one mob boss who truly ruled the city: Capone. Born in Brooklyn, New York, in 1899, Capone was the son of Italian immigrants. He was a good

Gibson Girls and Flappers

Prior to the 1920s many women aspired to achieve the image of the Gibson Girl, a young woman who dressed demurely, wore her long hair piled high atop her head, and devoted herself to husband and children. This image was frequently found in newspaper and magazine illustrations drawn by artist Charles Dana Gibson, who first created the Gibson Girl in the 1880s.

By the 1920s many women decided they did not want to be Gibson Girls but, rather, flappers. The flapper dressed in short skirts, wore her hair in a short bob, and enjoyed drinking, smoking cigarettes, and dancing until the early hours of the morning. The term *flapper* originated in Great Britain and was applied to young girls who wore their galoshes open, causing them to flap about as they walked.

The most famous flapper of the era was probably Zelda Fitzgerald, wife of novelist F. Scott Fitzgerald, who provided this definition of the flapper: "She flirted because it was fun to flirt and wore a one-piece bathing suit because she had a good figure, she covered her face with paint and powder because she didn't need it and she refused to be bored chiefly because she wasn't boring. She was conscious that the things she did were the things she always wanted to do."

Quoted in Valerie Weber and Helen Dryer, eds., *America in the 20th Century: 1920–1929.* Tarrytown, NY: Marshall Cavendish, 2003, p. 374.

student in elementary school—earning mostly Bs in his subjects—but he dropped out of school at age 14 after striking a teacher. Spending his time on the streets, it did not take long for Capone to come under the influence of neighborhood mobsters. He soon struck up a relationship with Frankie Yale, a ruthless killer and extortionist who hired him to run a bar he owned in Brooklyn. One night Capone got into an argument with a bar patron, who slashed him across the face with a knife. Capone would carry the scar for the rest of his life and would eventually become known in the headlines as "Scarface" Al Capone.

Capone left Brooklyn in 1919; he was summoned to Chicago by Johnny Torrio, a friend and fellow tough guy who had shifted his business to the Illinois city at the invitation of his uncle, James "Big Jim" Colosimo, head of the Chicago underworld. Colosimo's main business was prostitution, but once Prohibition arrived Torrio had big plans. The first order of business was to get rid of Colosimo—the old boss was found dead with two bullet holes in his head. No one was ever charged with the murder, but Torrio was the chief suspect.

With Colosimo out of the way, Torrio put his talents toward organizing the bootleg trade. He also made Capone his chief lieutenant. Together, Capone and Torrio planned to take over the Chicago rackets, eliminating their competitors in bloody shootouts. In 1925 Torrio ordered the murder of rival bootlegger Dion O'Banion; three men carried out the hit, gunning down O'Banion in a flower store he owned. Soon after the murder, two of O'Banion's lieutenants, Moran and Earl "Hymie Weiss" Wojciechowski, vowed to avenge the death of their boss. They cornered Torrio, seriously wounding the mob kingpin. Torrio recovered but decided he had had enough of the rackets. He retired to Italy, leaving Capone in charge of the criminal organization the two men had forged.

Ruler of the Chicago Rackets

Now in charge, Capone launched a ruthless campaign to take over the Chicago rackets. Wojciechowski was gunned down on a Chicago street in broad daylight. "Hymie Weiss is dead because he was a bull-head,"[21] Capone told reporters. Rather than fight on, the surviving members of Wojciechowski's gang agreed to join Capone's mob. Other local mobsters also gave in, agreeing to let Capone call the shots. But some refused and resolved to fight on. Moran insisted on maintaining his independence and refused to join Capone's mob—a decision that Moran and seven unfortunate members of his gang would eventually regret.

Capone was as much of a jazz fan as the mobsters in New York. He even opened his own version of the Cotton Club in Cicero, a small town just outside Chicago, and paid top dollar so that the best jazz musicians would play in his club. "Scarface got along with the musicians," recalled Hines. "He liked to come into a club with his henchmen and have the band play his requests. He was free with $100 tips."[22]

By the late 1920s Capone was the unquestioned ruler of the Chicago rackets, winning the crown through the relentless elimination of his enemies. As king of the Chicago underworld, he relished the publicity that accompanied every mob hit. After one rival mobster was found gunned down in the street, reporters asked Capone whether he was responsible. "I've been accused of every death except the casualty list of the World War,"[23] he shrugged.

A few weeks after the Saint Valentine's Day Massacre, the new president, Herbert Hoover, took office in the White House. He decided he had read enough in the newspapers about Capone and the Chicago rackets and directed federal agents to find a way to put Capone in jail. "Have you got this fellow Capone yet?"[24] he would often demand of his aides.

Downfall of a Mob Boss

The job fell to Elliot Ness, a 26-year-old federal agent who had been appointed to head a task force that targeted bootleggers. Ness recruited a team of incorruptible agents whose honesty was well known in law enforcement circles. When Capone learned of this special squad, he sent three of his gang members to bribe Ness and two of his deputies, offering the agents $2,000 each. Ness and the others refused the bribes. Ness then called a press conference and announced, "Possibly it wasn't too important for the world to know that we couldn't be bought, but I did want Al Capone and every gangster in the city to realize that there were still a few law enforcement agents who couldn't be swerved from their duty."[25] The newspapers dubbed Ness's squad the "Untouchables" because they could not be tainted by mob money. Ness led a series of highly publicized raids on illegal breweries, liquor warehouses, and other mob-owned establishments, often using a snowplow to burst through the doors. His campaign put a serious dent in Capone's business.

Meanwhile, other federal agents were looking very closely at Capone's tax records. After a decade of raking in millions of dollars in profits in the illegal alcohol business, federal agents were able to make a case of tax evasion against the mobster. In 1931 federal prosecutors indicted Capone on 22 counts of tax evasion, alleging that he owed more than $200,000 in unpaid taxes.

Capone went on trial in October 1931. Despite attempts by the mob boss to pack the jury with his cohorts, he was quickly convicted and sentenced to 11 years in prison. He began his prison sentence in 1932 and ultimately served seven years, spending most of his incarceration at the Alcatraz maximum security prison in San Francisco Bay. In ill health after his release, Capone would never again be an influential figure in American crime. He died quietly in bed in 1947 at the age of 48.

For many Americans, the Roaring Twenties was an era of music, dancing, drinking, and gay times—it was truly the Jazz Age. But beneath this veneer of gaiety and parties lurked mob kingpins like Capone, Torrio, Luciano, and others. Alcohol may have fueled these good times, but it took ruthless criminals to provide the beer and liquor to a public that did not seem to care how it was supplied or who died in the mob wars to control the notorious bootleg empires of the 1920s.

Chapter 3

Decade of Achievement and Discovery

B y today's standards the flight of Charles Lindbergh would be regarded as a modest achievement: He was the first aviator to fly nonstop across the Atlantic Ocean. His tiny plane, the *Spirit of St. Louis*, was powered by a single engine. He embarked from a small airport near New York City on the morning of May 20, 1927, arriving at Le Bourget Airport in Paris, France, $33^1/_2$ hours later. He flew a total distance of 3,614 miles (5,816km). Today's jet airliners cover the same distance in about 8 hours, and passengers enjoy dinner and a movie en route.

But in the 1920s aviation was still very much a new and untested mode of transportation. By the time of Lindbergh's feat, engine-powered flight was not yet 25 years old. Jet engines had yet to be developed—all aircraft were propeller driven. During the Great War a decade before, airplanes were proved to be effective weapons, but the pilots who flew them were fearless daredevils who risked their lives aboard the flimsy crafts. By the 1920s the engineering of the planes had improved, but flying was still regarded as a risky venture.

The Lindbergh flight was a tremendous feat, but it is only one of many impressive achievements and discoveries that would dominate newspaper headlines throughout the decade of the 1920s. Advancements were also achieved in the production of automobiles, as the vehicles became more reliable, affordable, and available to many Americans.

Meanwhile, though, some Americans resisted scientific advancement. In a small town in Tennessee, the scientific proof behind the evolution of the human race was put to the test in what was arguably the trial of the century.

Flight to France

The achievement that stands out most during the 1920s is the Lindbergh flight. In 1919 New York hotel owner Raymond Orteig offered $25,000 to anybody who could fly nonstop to Paris. Many prominent aviators accepted the challenge, but all were sidetracked as they made their attempts—some by technical difficulties that grounded their planes, others by crashes that caused injuries and even deaths.

In the American aviation community, Lindbergh was hardly a pilot of renown—he was employed by a St. Louis, Missouri, airline that held a contract to carry the US mail. But he convinced his boss and other investors to put up $17,000 for the venture, mainly to finance the construction of a specially designed airplane to make the crossing.

The shy Lindbergh hoped to make the flight with little fanfare, but word of the attempt leaked out. Just hours after the flight commenced, 40,000 spectators attending a boxing match at Yankee Stadium in New York observed a moment of silence for the brave aviator as he embarked on this most dangerous of missions. As the boxers prepared to square off, referee Joe Humphries signaled for the public address microphone to be brought into the ring. "Ladies and gentleman," he called out, "I want you to rise to your feet and think about a boy up there tonight who is carrying the hopes of all true-blooded Americans. Say a little prayer for Charles Lindbergh."[26]

Lindbergh's plane was stripped down to a minimum weight so it could carry a maximum amount of fuel. To lighten its weight, the plane was not equipped with a radio or even gauges. Lindbergh even elected to save a few pounds by refusing to take along a parachute. It seemed a parachute would be of little use if he had to bail out over the deep and icy Atlantic.

With no radio Lindbergh would be out of communication with the rest of the world for the entire length of the long, lonely flight. Later, Lindbergh wrote of the journey:

> Looking ahead at the unbroken horizon and limitless expanse of water, I'm struck by my arrogance in attempting such a flight. I'm giving up a continent, and heading out to sea in the most fragile vehicle ever devised by man. Why should I be so certain that a swinging compass needle will lead me to land and safety? Why have I dared stake my life on the belief that by drawing a line on paper . . . I can find my way through shifting air to Europe? Why have I been so sure that I can hold the nose of the *Spirit of St. Louis* on an unmarked point on that uniform horizon and find Nova Scotia, and Newfoundland, and Ireland, and finally an infinitesimal spot on the earth's surface called Le Bourget?[27]

He endured poor flying conditions. Rain and sleet pelted the tiny plane. An expert pilot, Lindbergh maneuvered through the ice and rain, climbing above the inclement weather. After a long day and night, he looked down and saw the unmistakable landmass of Ireland. A short time later the plane crossed the English Channel and then passed over France. At 9:52 p.m. on May 21, he sighted the Eiffel Tower and flew toward the famous Paris landmark. As he circled the tower, the lights of Paris glared below. In a state of euphoria, Lindbergh suddenly realized he was lost—he could not find the airport.

Lindbergh knew Le Bourget Airport was northeast of the city. He headed in that direction, aiming toward a dim, black square of land surrounded by light, guessing that it was the airport. He had guessed right. Gently, he eased the *Spirit of St. Louis* to a touchdown on the Le Bourget runway. He spotted a group of hangars and planned to taxi the plane toward them but suddenly realized a huge crowd had broken through police lines and was rushing the plane. He quickly brought the plane to a stop and, with the engine killed, heard the crowd shouting, "Lindbergh! Lindbergh! Lindbergh!" An estimated crowd of 150,000 had come to the airport to witness the historic landing.

Charles Lindbergh flew nonstop across the Atlantic Ocean, from New York City to Paris, in 1927 in a single-engine plane—a remarkable feat for the time. His historic flight was one of many important technological achievements of the decade.

Birth of the Space Program

Lindbergh's flight helped prove that aviation could be safe and reliable. Aviation suddenly attracted widespread interest from investors and business leaders who sought to establish passenger-carrying airlines. Among the first was Pan American World Airways, which formed within a year of Lindbergh's flight. Pan Am started by delivering mail from Key West, Florida, to Havana, Cuba, but soon added passenger service as well.

While aviation engineers were finding ways to make airplanes fly higher and longer, a different type of flight was under study: On March 16, 1926, scientist Robert Goddard launched the first liquid-fueled rocket from his aunt's farm in Auburn, Massachusetts.

It soared a mere 41 feet (12.5m) into the sky, traveling just 184 feet (56m) across a farm field. The flight lasted a total of 2.5 seconds. "The rocket did not rise at first, but the flame came out, and there was a steady roar," Goddard later wrote. "After a number of seconds it rose, slowly until it cleared the frame, and then at express-train speed, curving over to the left, and striking the ice and snow, still going at a rapid rate. It looked almost magical as it rose."[28]

Goddard's tiny rocket weighed just 10 pounds (4.5kg). And yet, from this most humble of beginnings, the US space program was born. Thirty-two years after the flight of Goddard's rocket, the United States would launch America's first unmanned satellite into earth orbit. That achievement would be followed by the first manned spaceflight and, in 1969, the successful landing of American astronauts on the moon. Later the Space Shuttle program, as well as the flights of unmanned satellites to other planets, would help accomplish many scientific feats and provide discoveries about the makeup of the stars and planets. All of those missions into space would be launched by employing the techniques of rocket thrust pioneered by Goddard on his aunt's farm in 1926.

Americans Become Car Owners

Goddard estimated that his rocket traveled at 60 miles per hour (96.6kph). That rate of speed would have hardly been impressive to Frank Lockhart. Just a few months after the flight of Goddard's rocket, Lockhart won the 1926 Indianapolis 500, driving his car at speeds in excess of 100 miles per hour (161kph). The race illustrated America's new love: the automobile.

By the 1920s, cars had been in production for decades; several car companies in Europe and America were manufacturing automobiles. However, they were built one at a time by engineers and craftspeople. They also tended to be expensive, well out of reach of the average American.

Henry Ford revolutionized the car industry when he devised a method of building cars on an assembly line. Under Ford's concept, each worker performed a specific job on the line—welding on the fenders, mounting the engine, installing the drive shaft, and so on. Ford envisioned a low-cost auto that could be sold to average Americans. In 1909, the first year the Ford Model T went into production, it took 12 hours to assemble the car. By 1927, the last year the Model T was manufactured, a new car rolled off Ford's assembly line every 24 seconds. In

A New Era in Movies

The 1920s represented an era of explosive growth in the film industry. At the start of the decade, the West Coast was already emerging as the movie capital of America. Large studios established filmmaking facilities in California, and due to the public's insatiable appetite for movies, many of them churned out dozens of titles a week. The top stars of the era were comedians Charlie Chaplin and Harold Lloyd, movie cowboys Tom Mix and William S. Hart, action star Douglas Fairbanks, heartthrob Rudolph Valentino, and girl-next-door Mary Pickford. These actors were all stars of the silent cinema—at the time engineers had not yet found a way to merge audio with film.

That would change in 1927 with the premiere of the film *The Jazz Singer*. Starring singer Al Jolson, the film was not quite a "talkie." The film included a few brief seconds of spoken dialogue only, but the film's many songs were vocalized. Audiences immediately embraced the film, and in a very short time, the silent era of Hollywood was over. Meanwhile, in 1928 animator Walt Disney produced the brief cartoon feature *Steamboat Willie* starring Mickey Mouse, establishing a character and mode of entertainment that have never lost their appeal.

the 18 years in which the Model T was in production, the Ford Motor Company sold some 15 million. And the Model T certainly was affordable: In its last year of production, a new Model T was priced at $350, whereas a used one was typically available for $60. This price range made the Model T the cheapest car on the market during the era and widely affordable by America's growing middle class.

Other companies copied Ford's production methods. Chryslers, Buicks, Cadillacs, Lincolns, Oldsmobiles, Dodges, Hudsons, Pierce Arrows, Durants, and dozens of other makes dominated narrow city streets and could also be found on dirt roads in the countryside. Surveying the industrial landscape of the 1920s that he helped create, Ford once boasted, "I invented the modern age."[29]

Model Ts park in a row outside of city hall in St. Louis, Missouri, circa 1920. The 1920s saw the rise in popularity of the Ford Model T. Its affordable price made it accessible to the country's growing middle class.

The Birth of TV

Another product that went into mass production in the 1920s was the radio. Radios were a common but unreliable form of communication, mostly because they were powered by batteries. When the batteries lost power, so did the radios. In 1922 the American Appliance Company developed a radio that could be powered by house current—in other words, it could be plugged into a wall socket. That development revolutionized the production of radios. By 1929 more than 10 million Americans owned radios; each day they tuned in to hear the news or listen to broadcasts of sports, concerts, comedies, dramas, and game shows. When Lindbergh landed in Paris, most Americans learned of the news through radio news bulletins.

Although radio would continue to be the nation's most important medium of communication for many years, research was under way in a laboratory in San Francisco, California, to transmit images over the airwaves. Engineer Philo T. Farnsworth developed a vacuum tube that could capture light and dark impulses transmitted over the airwaves. On September 27, 1927, Farnsworth transmitted the first television signal—the image was the glow of a lamp that was transmitted from one room to another.

From that first transmission, TV would grow into the dominant form of communication that it is today. It would take decades, though, before television sets would become available as consumer products at costs people could afford. Such companies as General Electric, Radio Corporation of America (later to be known as RCA), and Westinghouse would recognize the potential of television, and by the 1950s TV sets were finding their way into American homes, while entertainment companies produced programming for the new medium.

The Monkey Trial

While many people embraced the discoveries made by scientists and industrialists like Farnsworth, Ford, and Goddard, others resisted the advancement of science. In no case was this more evident than in Dayton, Tennessee, where in 1925 high school teacher John T. Scopes went on trial for breaking a state law that prohibited the teaching of the theory of evolution.

The concept was explained in 1859 by British naturalist Charles Darwin. In his book, *On the Origin of Species*, Darwin suggested that all life evolved through a process he labeled natural selection. According to Darwin, all living things are in a constant struggle for survival, and as the generations come and go, they pass on to their offspring the traits that have enabled them to survive. Therefore, Darwin claimed the surviving species undergo physical changes over long periods of time and may, eventually, even become new species. In other words, any species of plant or animal living in the twenty-first century might be far different from an ancestor that existed hundreds of thousands—or even millions—of years ago.

This theory enraged religious fundamentalists, who believe in a literal interpretation of the Bible (meaning they believe every word of Scripture should be accepted as fact). According to that interpretation, all living things appear today as God originally created them—just as the Bible suggested in the book of Genesis: "And God made the beast of the earth after his kind, and cattle after their kind, and every thing that creepeth upon the earth after his kind: and God saw that it was good. And God said, Let us make man in our image, after our likeness."

Two prominent individuals had made it their business to persuade state legislatures to outlaw the teaching of evolution. Fresh off their victory to enact the Eighteenth Amendment, William Jennings Bryan and Billy Sunday traveled the country, lobbying state lawmakers to ban the teaching of evolutionary science in schools. In Tennessee they succeeded when the legislature adopted the Butler Act, named for John Washington Butler, the lawmaker who introduced the measure.

One Tennessee business leader, coal mine owner George Rappleyea, believed evolution should be taught and sought a teacher to make a test case. He appealed to his friend Scopes, a Dayton biology teacher, to teach evolution in his class. Scopes agreed and was soon charged with violating the Butler Act.

Bryan announced he would personally prosecute Scopes and headed to Dayton to take over the case. Meanwhile, the American Civil Liberties Union hired the noted Chicago attorney Clarence Darrow to represent Scopes. And so, in this otherwise sleepy Tennessee town, one of the most high-profile trials of the twentieth century unfolded. During this trial two of the nation's most famous lawyers litigated the concept of whether humans were created in an unchangeable form by God or are capable of being transformed by a process called evolution. The press labeled it the "Monkey Trial," because Darwinists taught that apes are part of the evolutionary chain that leads to human beings.

Tarnished Beliefs

Fundamentalists flocked to Dayton to support Bryan and voice their support for the Bible. Reporters also flooded to Dayton to cover the trial, which received international press. Among the reporters covering the trial was H.L. Mencken, one of the most eloquent journalists of the era, whose dispatches were carried by his newspaper, the *Baltimore Evening Sun*. Of the scene in Dayton, he wrote:

> There was a friar wearing a sandwich sign announcing that he was the Bible champion of the world. There was a Seventh Day Adventist arguing that Clarence Darrow was the beast with seven heads and ten horns described in Revelation XIII, and that the end of the world was at hand. There was an ancient that maintained no Catholic could be Christian. There was the eloquent T.T. Martin of Blue Mountain, Mississippi, come to town with a truck-load of torches and hymn-books to put Darwin in his place. There was a singing brother bellowing apocalyptic hymns. There was William Jennings Bryan, followed everywhere by a gaping crowd. Dayton was having a roaring time. It was better than the circus.[30]

The trial opened on the sweltering morning of July 10. "Scopes is not on trial," Darrow declared early in the case. "Civilization is on trial."[31] Bryan countered that it was not Darwin or the Bible on trial—but that Scopes had clearly violated a law passed by the legislature of Tennessee.

The First Baseball Superstar

By the 1920s baseball was clearly in dire need of a hero. After the scandal of 1919, in which it was alleged that gambler Arnold Rothstein had bribed Chicago White Sox players to lose the World Series, many fans had soured on the sport. Soon, though, the sport would be saved by an unlikely hero. The rotund George Herman "Babe" Ruth Jr. hardly looked like an athlete, but he could hit a baseball harder and farther than anyone else playing the game.

Originally a pitcher, Ruth made his major league debut in 1914 with the Boston Red Sox. He proved to be one of the best pitchers in the American League, but the Red Sox found that he was even more valuable as a hitter. After an all-star career playing for the Red Sox, the New York Yankees bought his contract for the then-astounding sum of $100,000.

Playing for the Yankees, Ruth would accomplish feats unheard of in baseball. In 1920, his first year with the team, he hit 54 home runs—nearly double the previous record. In 1921 Ruth slugged 59 homers, and in 1927 the Sultan of Swat hit 60 home runs—a record that would stand for more than 30 years. Moreover, his career total of 714 homers would endure until 1974, when it was broken by Hank Aaron of the Atlanta Braves. And during his career with the Yankees, Ruth led his team to seven pennants and four World Series titles.

He insisted, "The right of the people speaking through the legislature, to control the schools which they create and support, is the real issue."[32]

Bryan called several of Scopes's students to the witness stand to testify that their teacher had taught Darwin's theory. Other townspeople took the stand as well, complaining that their children's beliefs in

God had been tarnished by Scopes. After leaving the witness stand, one teenager was overheard telling a friend, "I like him [Scopes], but I don't believe I came from a monkey."[33]

Expert Testimony

The highlight of the trial occurred when Bryan himself agreed to take the stand, testifying as an expert on the Bible. Under intense questioning by Darrow, Bryan declared that he was a staunch believer in such miracles as the creation of Eve from Adam's rib, the 40-day Great Flood, and the story of how Jonah was swallowed by the whale. "I am more interested in the Rock of Ages than the age of rocks,"[34] Bryan declared.

The trial ended after two weeks. The jury found Scopes in violation of the Butler Act. He was fined $100—Mencken's newspaper paid the fine. Darrow appealed the verdict; two years later the Tennessee Supreme Court reversed the verdict but upheld the Butler Act. In fact, the law prohibiting the teaching of evolution in Tennessee schools would not be repealed until 1967.

As for Bryan, he regarded the conviction of Scopes as a triumph and planned to make a national tour lecturing about the case. Five days after the trial, he attended services at a Methodist church, then enjoyed lunch with friends. After eating, he retired to his room for a nap. He died in his sleep.

More than Gangsters and Flappers

The Scopes trial was a rare exception in what was truly a progressive period of American history. The 1920s was an era of achievement and discovery. Advancements in aviation and industry, as well as the early research that would lead to spaceflight, television, and other technical marvels, occurred in the 1920s, proving that the decade was much more than an era of gangsters, flappers, and flagpole sitters.

Chapter 4

The Crash

During the 1920s Americans became familiar with an ominous phrase that many believed would threaten their freedom and prosperity: Red menace. This label referred to Communist agitators who pledged anarchy and called for the violent overthrow of the American government—a movement that had been brewing for years on the fringes of society.

Americans caught a glimpse of the Red menace in 1901 when President William McKinley was assassinated by Leon Czolgosz, an unemployed factory worker from Cleveland, Ohio, who had joined the anarchist movement. Czolgosz stalked McKinley at the Pan-American Exposition in Buffalo, New York. As McKinley mingled with the crowd, Czolgosz approached the president. When the president extended his hand to Czolgosz, the anarchist drew a gun and fired. He was convicted after a brief trial and executed three months later. "I killed the president because he was the enemy of the people—the good working people," Czolgosz declared. "I am not sorry for my crime."[35]

By the dawn of the 1920s, Americans had become fearful of that type of rhetoric and aimed to stamp out anarchy. On June 2, 1919, a major spark in the war against the Red menace was ignited when 9 bombs exploded outside the homes of several officials in Washington, DC. One of the bombs was detonated on the doorstep of the home of US attorney general A. Mitchell Palmer. Later, officials discovered another 30 bombs had been planted around the city, but they had failed to explode. Miraculously, nobody was killed, but other acts of anarchy did prove deadly: On September 16, 1920, an anarchist's bomb exploded on Wall Street in New York, killing 38 people and injuring hundreds more.

The fear of the Red menace illustrates that during the Roaring Twenties, while happy times may have been celebrated by the antics of flagpole sitters and flappers, there was also a dark side to the decade. Indeed, Americans would soon learn of scandal in the White House and panic on Wall Street.

The Palmer Raids

Palmer responded to the Red scare by declaring open war on anarchists. He ordered federal agents to round up all known anarchists—these raids on Communist cells became known as the Palmer raids. Among those arrested in the raids were Emma Goldman and her companion, Alexander Berkman. Goldman was the feminist leader who had endorsed Sigmund Freud's ideas supporting sexual freedom for women. She was also a Russian immigrant who was a vocal leader of the anarchist movement. Berkman was also a well-known Communist agitator. Taken into custody, Goldman and Berkman were deported to Russia. Later, Goldman wrote that her arrest and deportation were clearly in violation of her constitutional rights. She said:

> It has often been suggested to me that the Constitution of the United States is a sufficient safeguard for the freedom of its citizens. It is obvious that even the freedom it pretends to guarantee is very limited. I have not been impressed with the adequacy of the safeguard. The nations of the world, with centuries of international law behind them, have never hesitated to engage in mass destruction when solemnly pledged to keep the peace; and the legal documents in America have not prevented the United States from doing the same.[36]

She added that anarchy—the use of violence to oppose the government—is justified when circumstances demand an extreme response by the oppressed. She said, "When the failure of modern dictatorship and authoritarian philosophies becomes more apparent and the realization of failure more general, anarchism will be vindicated."[37]

Sacco and Vanzetti

Palmer's agents were given widespread authority to conduct the raids. In all, some 10,000 suspected Reds were rounded up and deported, including many who probably did not belong to anarchist movements. In rounding up the suspects, the agents barged into their homes without search warrants, often used violence to beat confessions out of suspects, and regularly tossed suspected anarchists into jail on flimsy evidence. As the raids got under way, William J. Flynn, head of the US Bureau of Investigation (the forerunner of the Federal Bureau of Investigation), told his chief aide, Frank Burke, "I leave it entirely to your discretion as to the methods by which you should gain access to [the homes of suspects]."[38]

Two men caught up in the campaign against anarchy were Italian immigrants Nicola Sacco and Bartolomeo Vanzetti, who were charged in 1920 with the theft of $15,000 from a factory near Boston as well as the murders of the paymaster and a guard. Both men were active in the anarchist movement, but both men insisted they were innocent of the robbery and murders. Federal prosecutors resorted to underhanded tactics to gather evidence. Indeed, the government placed spies in the prison where Sacco and Vanzetti were held, hoping to hear jailhouse confessions from the two men. A government-paid informer even rented a room in the boarding house run by Sacco's wife with the intent of hearing her make incriminating remarks. Perhaps worst of all, another government-paid informer joined the defense team of attorneys and investigators who were gathering evidence of the defendants' innocence.

The evidence presented during the trial was far from conclusive— 35 witnesses testified, and only one said he was certain he saw the

The 1920s in Rural America

Flappers, jazz musicians, and the prosperity brought by rising stock prices never quite made it to rural America during the 1920s. For farmers or sharecroppers, the Roaring Twenties were not an era of good times but, rather, often a time of toil and economic woes.

In states like North Carolina, many rural people left their farms to find jobs in city factories. As the cities grew larger, those who remained on the farms found themselves under pressure to produce more food to feed the hungry city dwellers. Overproduction of farm crops led to lower prices for corn, wheat, beef, pork, and other farm products.

As a result, an economic depression settled over rural America long before the stock market crashed. Elizabeth Gillespie McRae, assistant professor of history at Western Carolina University, explains:

> The Roaring Twenties was not a flush decade for the state's farmers. As agricultural overproduction drove prices down, a depression settled over the state's farms in the early 1920s. Many farmers lost their land. The number of tenant farmers—farmers who worked but did not own land—grew during the decade. In fact, the total wealth of North Carolinians actually fell during the Roaring Twenties.

Elizabeth Gillespie McRae, "How the Twenties Roared in North Carolina," *Tar Heel Junior Historian*, Spring 2004, p. 2.

two men at the scene of the crime. Throughout the case, Judge Webster Thayer could barely conceal his belief that the two men were guilty. Despite the grave miscarriage of justice reflected by the proceedings, on July 1, 1920, the jury convicted the two men of the robbery and murders. Thayer sentenced them to death, and Vanzetti later recalled:

> There was not a vibration of sympathy in his tone when he did so. I wondered as I listened to him, why he hated me so. Is not a judge supposed to be impartial? But now I think I know—I must have looked like a strange animal to him, being a plain worker, an alien, and a radical to boot. And why was it that all my witnesses, simple people who were anxious to tell the simple truth, were laughed at and disregarded? No credence was given to their words because they, too, were merely aliens.[39]

Sacco and Vanzetti remained on death row for seven years while their case was on appeal. Finally, their appeals exhausted, both men were executed on August 23, 1927.

The Scandals of President Harding

As newspaper readers followed the campaign against the anarchists, another important story was finding its way into the headlines. President Warren G. Harding may have promised a return to normalcy, but his administration was wracked by scandal. The president himself flaunted the Eighteenth Amendment, imbibing whiskey at public meetings. He also maintained an adulterous affair with Nan Britton, a young woman from Harding's hometown of Marion, Ohio.

But the major scandal of the Harding years did not involve drinking or adultery. Rather, the Teapot Dome scandal was found to involve bribery, misconduct in office, and misuse of public lands. In 1921 Harding appointed Albert Fall as secretary of the interior, a department charged with maintaining publicly owned lands. Fall was an unscrupulous character; rather than act as a responsible custodian of national parks and similar lands, he used his position for personal gain.

On May 21, 1921, Fall convinced Harding to approve the lease of federal lands at Teapot Dome, Wyoming, to oil speculator Harry Sinclair. Sinclair planned to erect derricks on the land to pump oil to help feed the growing national demand for gasoline. Fall had given Harding the phony story that unless the oil was pumped out, it would drain away on its own, polluting neighboring lands. The gullible Harding accepted the story without question. To repay Fall for the lucrative contract, Sinclair provided the interior secretary with a kickback of $70,000 in cash and $233,000 in US government bonds. Later, the value of the oil was estimated at several hundred million dollars.

Word of the deal leaked out almost immediately. When reporters asked Harding about the scandal, the president replied, "If Albert Fall isn't an honest man, I am not fit to be president of the United States."[40]

Silent Cal

Details of the scandal engulfed Washington over the next two years and dominated Harding's presidency. When Republican senator Robert M. La Follette of Wisconsin announced in April 1922 that he would lead an investigation into the scandal, his office was ransacked—allegedly by an agent working for Fall or Sinclair hoping to destroy evidence.

Harding had not benefited financially from the scandal, but the affair continued to dominate his presidency and affect his health. He suffered from depression for months, and on August 2, 1923, died of a heart attack. As for Fall and Sinclair, they were both convicted of crimes relating to the scandal and sentenced to prison terms.

Harding was succeeded in the White House by the vice president, Calvin Coolidge, who pledged to restore dignity to the presidency. The nation prospered under Coolidge, and he was easily elected to a full term as president in 1924. Around Washington, the new president was known as "Silent Cal," largely because he preferred to keep his opinions to himself. One of the most familiar stories of the era involved a prominent lady of Washington society who approached the president and said, "I made a bet today that I could get more than two words out of you." Coolidge replied, "You lose."[41]

Grip of Poverty

Not everybody shared in the prosperity of the 1920s. Many people were held in the grip of poverty, particularly in the rural South. The people who suffered most were African Americans. Their ancestors had been freed from slavery after the Civil War, but many southern whites refused to accept them as equals. By the 1920s Jim Crow laws barring African Americans from whites-only theaters, public restrooms, restaurants, and similar places were well established in southern states. It was during this era that the Ku Klux Klan grew in membership and influence, terrorizing blacks in the South and Midwest.

Hooded members of the Ku Klux Klan parade through Long Branch, New Jersey, in 1924. The Klan's membership and influence grew during the decade, especially in the South but also in parts of the Midwest and Northeast.

Elsewhere, dark clouds were gathering in Europe. In Italy the fascist Black Shirt movement under Benito Mussolini seized power in 1922. By 1925 Mussolini had established himself as a powerful dictator. In Germany the heavy reparations inflicted on the country by the winners of the Great War had taken their toll. During the early part of the decade, Germany was a land of chaos as all manner of ideologies—from communism to democracy to fascism—struggled to take control. Meanwhile, the country fell into a deep economic depression. Amid this chaos, the fascist Nazi Party led by the fanatical Adolf Hitler gained legitimacy among the German people and made plans to seize the government. Across the Pacific Ocean, a militaristic regime had taken power in Japan and soon drew up plans to expand its influence over other countries in Asia.

Buying Stock on Margin

For the vast majority of Americans, these troubles were of little concern as they enjoyed a wide measure of prosperity. Under the Harding and Coolidge administrations, America's biggest corporations were allowed to grow virtually free of government regulation. Indeed, it seemed as though anyone could be successful in business. In 1920 Walter Chrysler left his job as a factory manager for General Motors to start his own car company; by 1927 the Chrysler Corporation was selling nearly 200,000 cars a year. Another industry that flourished during the 1920s was the rubber industry, due to the demand for automobile tires. By the 1920s there were nearly 200 companies in the tire business, although 4 companies—Goodyear, B.F. Goodrich, Firestone, and US Rubber—controlled nearly half the market. Meanwhile, all manner of electrical appliances started appearing in people's homes. For example, electric toasters made their debut in home kitchens as far back as 1893, but it was not until 1926 that the Waters Genter Company added a timer to the machines, enabling people to make their morning slice of toast exactly the way they preferred. Electric vacuum cleaners had been invented in 1901, but in 1920 the

Air-Way Sanitizer Company of Toledo, Ohio, achieved a tremendous advancement in the devices when it found a way to equip them with disposable dust bags. According to the nation's political leaders, all of these advancements were possible because the government kept out of the way of business, imposing a minimum of regulations on commercial enterprise. In 1925 Coolidge gave a speech in which he declared, "The chief business of the American people is business."[42] Most Americans tended to agree—with the corporations enjoying huge profits, jobs were easy to come by.

The skyrocketing value of these companies was reflected in the worth of their stock sold on the New York Stock Exchange. Among the major beneficiaries were America's car manufacturers, whose factories ran nonstop making automobiles. In 1921 a share of the automaker Chrysler traded for $16. By 1928 that same share of stock was worth $563.

When Herbert Hoover was elected president in 1928, he made it clear that the government would continue to adhere to a policy of non-intervention in business. Declared Hoover, "We must not be misled by the claim that the source of all wisdom is in the government."[43]

As political leaders like Coolidge and Hoover pledged to keep out of the way of American business, investors continued to bid up the value of corporate stock at a frenzied pace. Many people took advantage of the government's lack of regulation to buy shares of stock on margin. Buying on margin meant the customers did not have to pay cash for the stock. Instead, they were essentially receiving IOUs from their stock-brokers, who kept a record of the sales in the margins of the purchase orders. After selling the stock and cashing in, the investors would pay off their debts to their brokers.

For investors, it was a golden era—a time when virtually every investment paid off in big returns. Said economist John Kenneth Galbraith, "Never had there been a better time to get rich, and people knew it. 1928, indeed, was the last year in which Americans were buoyant, uninhibited, and utterly happy. It wasn't that 1928 was too good to last; it was only that it didn't last."[44]

Hundreds of unemployed New Yorkers line up for food rations at Times Square during the Great Depression. Frenzied selling of overpriced stock that lost value day by day began in October 1929. When the market finally bottomed out in 1932, it left behind a trail of financial ruin.

Stock Tips from Elevator Operators

The system of buying on margin worked well as long as the value of the stock continued to rise. But if the stock dropped in value, investors would owe their brokers more than the value of the stock they bought on margin. A big drop, from $100 a share to $10 a share, for instance, would mean the client would owe the broker $90 per share of stock. If the client owned 1,000 shares, the loss would be tremendous. Even wealthy people would find it difficult to meet their margin payments under these circumstances.

There was another calamity brewing in the market: Dabbling in the stock market had become so widespread that it seemed nearly everyone fancied themselves expert investors. Many ordinary people with little knowledge of how the stock market actually works freely dispensed tips to their friends and others. This type of speculation increased the value of many companies, including those that did not have bright prospects ahead of them. In other words, their value was very much overinflated. Amateur stock experts had no way of knowing these facts—they gave out tips based on rumor and innuendo. The comic movie star Groucho Marx was known to be particularly gullible—he often accepted stock tips from elevator operators. "What an easy racket,"[45] he once declared.

Throughout much of the 1920s, stock prices continued to spiral upward. On the first trading day after Labor Day in 1929, the value of the stock market reached an all-time high. On October 22, 1929, economist Irving Fisher predicted the boom would continue. He said, "The nation is marching along a permanently high plateau of prosperity."[46]

Panic Selling

Fisher made those comments two days before the sun rose on October 24, 1929—a day that would become known as Black Thursday. On that date, traders started selling overpriced shares of stock. Seeing prices drop, many investors dumped their shares, worried that they would not be able to pay their brokers for their margin buys. By the end of the day, the market lost 9 percent of its value.

Black Thursday was followed five days later by Black Tuesday, in which the market suffered a 13 percent drop in just a few hours of trading. Panic selling gripped the market and dominated trading over the next several months. The market finally reached bottom in 1932—by

The Stock Market Crash and Suicide

Popular opinion holds that the 1929 stock market crash caused a wave of suicides by investors who lost their life savings—particularly by investors who lived in New York City, the financial capital of America. Statistics suggest that is a myth. According to statistics compiled by the US Department of Commerce, the suicide rate in New York City in 1929 was 17 victims per 100,000 residents—only a slight increase over the previous year's statistic of nearly 16 victims per 100,000 residents.

Still, there is no question that some people took their lives when they learned their savings were wiped out. One of the suicide victims was the grandfather of filmmaker Roger Graef. "My grandfather was not a captain of industry," Graef said. "He was selling insurance. . . . He was a sad man who was trying to make his way, support his family, had invested in Wall Street with the hope and belief that that was going to do what he wanted to do which was create a safe and better future for his children."

Another suicide victim was W.J. Keyes, an executive with a radio manufacturing company. Before jumping out of a window of a New York skyscraper, Keyes left a suicide note that said, "Last April I was worth $100,000. Today I am $24,000 in the hole."

Roger Graef, "My Grandfather Killed Himself in the 1929 Crash," BBC News, October 6, 2008. http://news.bbc.co.uk.

Quoted in Tom Shachtman, *The Day America Crashed: A Narrative Account of the Great Stock Market Crash of October 24, 1929*. New York: Putnam, 1979, p. 98.

then the American stock market had lost nearly 90 percent of its value. Marx, whose personal fortune was wiped out by the market crash, was somehow able to find humor in it all. "I was a wealthy man on the eighteenth hole of a golf course," he quipped. "By the time I got to the clubhouse I was destitute."[47]

Many Americans faced financial ruin. A long period of economic decline known as the Great Depression soon swept through America. In 1930, as the nation headed toward economic doldrums, the unemployment rate stood at 3 percent. Within three years, the unemployment rate would rise to 25 percent—idling one out of every four American workers.

People who had known only prosperity found themselves scratching for pennies or seeking charity. Robert Hasting grew up in Marion, Illinois, in the years following the crash. He recalled that on Saturday mornings the local dairy, in an act of charity, would sell a bucket of skim milk for a nickel. Each Saturday, Hastings's mother gave him a nickel and sent him to the dairy. "I held our enamel water bucket in one gloved hand and a nickel in the other," he says. "I took my place in the long line. It was unbelievable. When your turn came, regardless of how big your bucket, you held it under the faucet of the big, stainless drum while that great white river just ran and ran."[48]

In the cities many people—unable to pay rent—were kicked out of their apartments and forced to live on the streets. Many of them sought shelter in public places such as railroad stations as a way of keeping warm during the winter months. Others lived in shantytowns in shacks made of scraps of wood, tin, packing crates, and whatever else was handy. One New Yorker, Robert Bendiner, recalled, "Dozens of such colonies sprung up in the city—along the two rivers, in the empty lots of the Bronx, and on the flats of Brooklyn, but not nearly enough to accommodate the swelling army of the dispossessed."[49]

Dictators Come to Power

The Great Depression was not limited to the United States. Other countries suffered as well, in large part because of the crumbling state of the American economy. Fearing a shortage of raw materials, American companies began hoarding resources, which reduced the supply of raw materials available to European countries and Japan. As a result, unemployment, poverty, hunger, and hopelessness struck many of these countries particularly hard.

Amid the suffering in Europe, despotic leaders made grand promises to rescue their citizens from their hardships. In reality these leaders harbored schemes of conquest. In Japan the militaristic regime would soon strike against China and Manchuria. As men like Hitler and Mussolini as well as Hideki Tojo in Japan seized control of their countries and smashed their opponents, Americans could not ignore the ominous clouds of war gathering on the horizon. With such dark times ahead, it was clear that the fun times of the Roaring Twenties had come to a close.

Chapter 5

What Is the Legacy of the Roaring Twenties?

Even Lucky Luciano understood the implications of the stock market crash. Watching the country plummet into the depths of the Great Depression, Luciano knew the days of Prohibition were numbered. "The public won't buy it no more," he told his gang members. "When they ain't got nothin' else, they gotta have a drink or there's gonna be trouble. And they're gonna want to have that drink legal."[50]

Despite more than a decade of breaking up bootlegging rings, closing down speakeasies, and nabbing rumrunners, federal agents had hardly put a dent in the illegal alcohol business. Clearly, Prohibition had failed; it had always been an unpopular law. In Philadelphia, bootleg czar Max "Boo Boo" Hoff presided over an empire of 13,000 speakeasies. Hoff was known as one of the nation's primary suppliers of grain alcohol—the vital ingredient of bootleg liquor. Throughout the 1920s Hoff shipped some 350,000 gallons (1.3 million L) of grain alcohol to illegal distilleries throughout the country.

Hoff paid monthly bribes totaling $10,000 to one high-ranking Philadelphia police official. Other members of the Philadelphia police also received monthly stipends for letting Hoff run his bootleg empire. "He is like a giant spider in the middle of a great web with eyes in front and behind," Philadelphia district attorney John Monaghan said of Hoff. "A man who sees everything, knows everything and controls everything in the underworld."[51]

Repeal of Prohibition

The hardships of the Great Depression had left Americans in a dismal mood. Congress and state legislators nationwide responded to that mood in 1933 with ratification of the Twenty-First Amendment to the US Constitution, repealing Prohibition. The amendment left it up to the states to decide for themselves whether they would be "dry" or "wet."

States enacted their own laws regulating the sales of alcoholic beverages to conform with the moral standards of their citizens. Some states passed legislation outlawing alcohol sales and consumption. These laws proved to be widely unenforceable. If someone in a dry state desired a drink and lived next door to a wet state, all that person had to do was step across the state line. Among the last holdouts were Oklahoma, which maintained a ban on alcohol through 1959, and Mississippi, which finally repealed its prohibition on alcohol in 1966.

Some states left the decision up to their individual county governments. By 2010—nearly 80 years after the repeal of Prohibition—328 county governments in eight states still did not allow restaurants to serve drinks or stores to sell beer, liquor, or wine, although residents of those counties were permitted to enjoy alcoholic beverages in the privacy of their homes. Meanwhile, some county governments have left the decision on alcohol sales in the hands of individual towns and cities. One of the towns that elected to stay dry is tiny Winona, Texas, which has a population of about 600 people. "It almost seems like we're behind the times,"[52] admits Winona mayor Rusty Smith. Still, under Winona's town ordinance, no commercial establishment is permitted to sell alcohol, either by the drink or by the bottle.

Although the federal government has determined that alcohol sales is an issue best decided on the state and local levels, Congress has addressed the issue of underage drinking. Following the repeal of Prohibition, states set their own minimum drinking ages—all were set between 18 and 21. But in 1984 Congress reacted to the growing problem of drunk driving and underage drinking by adopting the National Minimum Drinking Age Act, which set 21 as a national minimum legal age for purchasing and consuming alcoholic beverages.

Americans celebrate the repeal of Prohibition in 1933. The Twenty-First Amendment, repealing the ban on the sale and consumption of alcoholic beverages, left it up to states to decide whether to be "dry" or "wet."

March of the Bonus Army

The repeal of Prohibition was only one of the legislative changes made by the federal government in the aftermath of the Roaring Twenties. During the 1920s three US presidents—Harding, Coolidge, and Hoover—pledged that government would not intrude in people's lives, but the arrival of the Great Depression changed that attitude. Hoover reacted to the Great Depression by recommending that the US government sponsor a number of public works programs—such as the construction of roads, bridges, and dams—to provide jobs to unemployed

Americans. He also pledged federal assistance to prop up the small community banks, which were failing in large numbers. When these banks failed, their depositors—largely middle-class Americans—lost their life savings.

As conditions grew worse, in the spring of 1932 thousands of veterans of the Great War marched on Washington, DC, demanding bonuses they claimed they were owed by the federal government. They set up shacks in a swampy part of the city along the Anacostia River. Many of these veterans, members of the self-proclaimed Bonus Army, aimed to stay until Hoover agreed to pay the bonuses.

Each day, newspapers and newsreel cameras recorded their plight. Finally, in July Hoover ordered the US Army to intervene and tear down the shacks. Soldiers entered the Bonus Army's shantytown brandishing rifles fixed with bayonets. Using teargas, they pushed back the veterans. To millions of people at home watching the newsreel footage of the siege and reading about the treatment of these war veterans in their hometown newspapers, it appeared as though Hoover felt little empathy for the plight of the veterans or any Americans suffering through the Depression.

In fact, Hoover continued to maintain that the Depression was a temporary setback and that the American economy was still fundamentally healthy. He stuck to his principles that government should keep out of the way of private business, giving corporations the opportunities to recover on their own. Says economist Herbert Feis, "Hoover could not grasp or would not face the hard realities which called for deviations from principles and practices that he deemed essential to American greatness and freedom."[53] As things grew worse, Hoover remained in the White House, refusing to see for himself the signs of economic distress that were gripping the country.

From the New Deal to the Tea Party

In the election of 1932, with millions out of work and the truly destitute living in shantytowns derisively known as "Hoovervilles," the incumbent president was booted out of office in a landslide. The new president, Franklin D. Roosevelt, pledged a New Deal for Americans. No longer would the government maintain a hands-off policy—now the government would be a driving force in nearly everyone's lives. Roosevelt had been a major advocate for the repeal of Prohibition—he intended to tax the sales of alcoholic beverages and use the income to finance his New Deal programs.

Under Roosevelt, the government established a number of programs designed to employ people in public works projects while also ensuring them an income after retirement. In 1935 Congress passed the Social Security Act. Under the act, American workers contribute a portion of their paychecks to a federal fund that provides them with pensions upon retirement. Social Security has provided older Americans with a vital source of income. By the dawn of the twenty-first century, many experts were predicting that longer life expectancies for Americans might work against the Social Security program. They warn that it will not be able to afford to keep paying benefits to people as they grow older. By 2011 the debate over how to fund Social Security turned fierce. Many members of Congress have proposed raising the age at which Americans can start receiving their Social Security benefits, while others steadfastly oppose the proposal.

As for everything else the government does for its individual citizens—from providing a military for protection to low-interest loans so students can afford college to health care for the indigent—it has all come under intense scrutiny. Some members of Congress feel the government has overreached and spends too much money on these services. Many of the programs under fire can trace their roots to Roosevelt's New Deal. However, many political leaders have pledged to return to the ideals of Harding, Coolidge, and Hoover, who believed government should have a limited role in the lives of Americans.

Some leaders of the modern Tea Party movement regard Coolidge as a hero. The Tea Party, which gained traction in American politics in 2010, is composed of political conservatives who believe government should have a limited role in people's lives. Says Andrew Hemingway, chair of the Tea Party group Liberty Caucus of New Hampshire, "The tea party's ideal presidential candidate would most likely be someone

Unemployment During the Great Depression

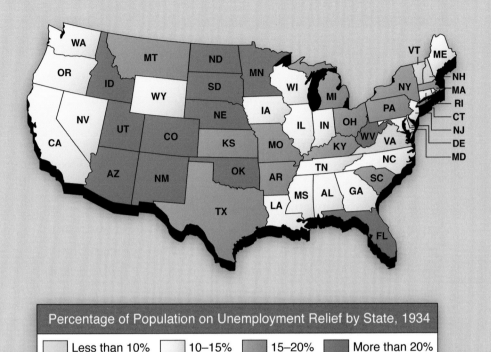

Percentage of Population on Unemployment Relief by State, 1934

Less than 10% | 10–15% | 15–20% | More than 20%

who combines the right political principles of limited government with a self-effacing approach to the wielding of power—and an aversion to the trappings of the office. . . . The tea party movement clearly wants a candidate like President Calvin Coolidge."[54]

Regulating the Stock Market

One place where government intervention is evident is regulation of the American stock market. In 1934 Congress created the US Securities and Exchange Commission (SEC) specifically to prevent a repeat of the 1929 crash. The SEC has established strict rules that govern the trading of stocks. Many of those rules apply to margin trading. Among those rules are requirements for investors to establish accounts with

The Rise and Fall of the Ku Klux Klan

The original Ku Klux Klan formed in the wake of the Civil War. Organized by veterans of the Confederate army, the racist Klan terrorized blacks, kidnapping and often murdering them through lynchings. By the late 1800s the Klan had disappeared.

In 1915 William Simmons, an alcoholic preacher from Georgia, reformed the Ku Klux Klan, naming himself head of the organization—the Imperial Wizard. Simmons's robed and hooded group of racists stumbled along for five years without much support, but in 1920 he hired two expert organizers, Edward Clarke and Elizabeth Tyler. Clarke and Tyler used their skills to raise money, recruit members, and garner publicity.

By 1921 the Klan had more than 100,000 members and was raising about $40,000 a month in dues. "We are a movement of the plain people, very weak in the matter of culture, intellectual support, and trained leadership," declared Hiram Wesley Evans, who took over as Imperial Wizard in 1922.

During the 1920s the Klan elected members to Congress and gave support to other members of the House and Senate, as well as several governors and numerous state legislators. The Klan's influence on American politics was significant. Not until the civil rights movement of the 1950s and 1960s would African Americans begin to enjoy the rights guaranteed to all Americans. Today the Klan still exists, but thanks to the adoption of hate crime laws and the vigilance of prosecutors, the organization has been reduced to a fringe group with few dedicated followers.

Quoted in Nathan Miller, *New World Coming: The 1920s and the Making of Modern America*. Cambridge, MA: Da Capo, 2003, p. 144.

their brokers to cover their losses in the event stock prices drop. Also, the SEC has set limits on the number of shares that can be purchased on margin. In 1933 Congress also took steps to protect bank deposits, establishing the Federal Deposit Insurance Corporation, which reimburses depositors should their banks fail.

In the years since the 1929 crash, the stock market has endured many volatile periods, sometimes losing billions of dollars in value on a single day. Nevertheless, because of government regulation of the stock market, there has never been another crash that could be equated to the debacle of October 1929.

As the government took steps to protect investors, it also took aim at the mobsters who had made fortunes during Prohibition. Following the repeal, the gangs that had been running the illegal alcohol trade found new enterprises. Many of them sponsored illegal sports betting—running bookie joints that take wagers on football games, horse racing, and other sports. Some of the gangs entered the lucrative narcotics trade. Some gangs went into the prostitution business. As these gangs prospered, organized crime grew into a major concern as powerful mobsters gained control over lucrative illegal activities.

Starting in the 1970s lawmakers enacted measures designed specifically to break up criminal organizations. Among them is the Racketeer Influenced and Corrupt Organizations Act, or RICO. Under RICO it is a crime simply to belong to a mob, even if law enforcement officials are unable to link individual gangsters to specific crimes. Another important tool is the federal witness protection program, in which mob insiders are given new homes and identities in exchange for their testimony in court against crime kingpins. Also, advancements in electronic eavesdropping technology have given law enforcement agents valuable tools to spy on mobsters and gain evidence against them. In recent years federal agents have used these tools to convict and imprison such crime bosses as John Gotti of New York, Nicodemo Scarfo of Philadelphia, and James Marcello of Chicago. Certainly, organized crime still maintains a presence in twenty-first-century America, but now law enforcement agents have many tools at their disposal to break up these gangs.

Workers widen streets, circa 1935, under the Works Progress Administration (WPA) program created by President Franklin D. Roosevelt. Roosevelt established numerous programs to aid Americans whose lives and livelihoods were destroyed during the Great Depression.

The Downfall of a Mob Boss

As for Luciano, his reign finally ended in 1936 when he was convicted of running a prostitution ring—a charge Luciano vigorously denied. He was convicted through the efforts of Thomas Dewey, an ambitious prosecutor who would eventually serve as governor of New York and later run unsuccessfully for president. Luciano maintained that Dewey targeted him simply to garner headlines to enhance his political career.

Luciano was sentenced to 30 years in prison, to be spent in the dismal Dannemora Prison in upstate New York. He was paroled in 1946 but ordered deported to his native Italy. The ex-crime boss remained briefly in Italy, then sailed for Havana, Cuba, where he helped establish the Caribbean island as an entertainment mecca for wealthy American gamblers—a status the country maintained until Communist Fidel Castro seized power in 1959.

Luciano left Cuba long before Castro took over—the American government learned that the exiled mobster was living in Havana and pressured the government of dictator Fulgencio Batista to kick him out. Luciano was forced to return to Italy, where he lived out his life. He died in 1962.

World War Returns

In Europe and Asia a very different type of criminal was seizing power. The fascists who gained toeholds in their countries' politics during the 1920s gained widespread power during the 1930s. Adolf Hitler dreamed of dominating the entire European continent and in 1939 launched an invasion of Poland that touched off World War II. America was drawn into the war in 1941 when Hitler's allies, the Japanese, launched a surprise attack on the US Navy base at Pearl Harbor in Hawaii. The war in Europe lasted until May 1945, when advancing American and Russian troops overran the German capital of Berlin. Three months later the Japanese surrendered after President Harry Truman authorized the use of atomic bombs on the cities of Hiroshima and Nagasaki.

Following the war, the world's political leaders agreed to form the United Nations (UN). Similar to President Woodrow Wilson's concept for the League of Nations, the UN serves as a forum to solve international disputes. It has also authorized collective force to target despotic regimes. The UN has often exercised this power: In 2002 UN members authorized the use of force to oust Iraqi dictator Saddam Hussein.

In the years following World War II, America settled into an era of prosperity as returning veterans established homes and families. Beneath this veneer of prosperity, though, the angry voices of the civil rights movement could be heard. African Americans were no longer prepared to endure the state-sanctioned segregation imposed by the South's decades-old Jim Crow laws or the unwritten but understood racial rules of the northern states.

Many of the civil rights leaders of the 1950s and 1960s found inspiration in a group of African American writers, artists, and performers who were part of a 1920s movement known as the Harlem Renaissance. These creative people provided an important record of the black experience in America while also laying the intellectual groundwork for the future civil rights movement. Among the leaders of the Harlem Renaissance were poets Langston Hughes, Countee Cullen, and Arna Bontemps, novelists Wallace Thurman and Zora Neale Hurston, and actor and singer Paul Robeson. In 1926 Hughes published his first book of poetry, titled *The Weary Blues*. The book included the poem "I, Too," which addressed the Jim Crow experience faced by many American blacks.

The Lost Generation and the Vicious Circle

As writers such as Hughes and the other members of the Harlem Renaissance made their voices known, other American writers were also composing important works of literature. Following the Great War, many of the top American writers found their way to Paris. Among them were F. Scott Fitzgerald, Henry Miller, Gertrude Stein, and Ernest Hemingway. They became known as the "Lost Generation"—a generation of young people searching for the meaning of life in the wake of such horrific warfare. Among the works of literature produced during the 1920s were Hemingway's *The Sun Also Rises*, a story of war veterans putting their lives back together, and Fitzgerald's novel of the Jazz Age, *The Great Gatsby*.

Not all of America's top creative people were headquartered in Paris. During the 1920s a small group of America's top writers, including Dorothy Parker, Robert Benchley, George S. Kaufman, and Alexander Woollcott, met daily for lunch at the Algonquin Hotel in New York. Known as the Algonquin Round Table and, occasionally, the Vicious Circle, this group of wits and satirists was responsible for an enormous output of novels, plays, and screenplays during the 1920s. Kaufman's contributions to the Broadway stage included the comedies *Dulcy* (1921), *Merton of the Movies* (1922), *Beggar on Horseback* (1924), and

The Birth of the *New Yorker*

Many of the top writers of the 1920s published stories in the *New Yorker*, a magazine founded in 1925 by publisher Harold Ross. Ross sought to establish a sophisticated and witty chronicle of life in New York City. In a prospectus for investors, Ross announced that his new magazine would "not be edited for the old lady in Dubuque."

Over the next several decades, the magazine grew from a city journal into a publication of national interest and readership. It published the work of some of America's most important writers, including Ernest Hemingway, J.D. Salinger, Philip Roth, John Updike, and E.B. White. Shirley Jackson's story of small-town horror, "The Lottery," first appeared in the *New Yorker* in 1948. Today, "The Lottery" is regarded as required reading for many middle school English students. Another highlight was the magazine's publication of "Hiroshima," John Hersey's eyewitness account of the aftermath of the atomic bombing of the city of Hiroshima, Japan, which ended World War II. "Hiroshima" spanned the entire length of the magazine when it was published in 1946.

Today, the *New Yorker* remains a popular weekly magazine. In addition to commentary, political coverage, stories about culture, and book and movie reviews, the magazine publishes the art of America's top cartoonists. Among the cartoonists whose work has appeared in the *New Yorker* is the late Charles Addams, whose macabre comedy featuring the Addams family inspired a 1960s TV situation-comedy, two film comedies in the 1990s, and a 2011 Broadway musical.

Quoted in Jill Lapore, "Untimely: What Was at Stake in the Spat Between Henry Luce and Harold Ross?," *New Yorker*, April 19, 2010. www.newyorker.com.

The Butter and Egg Man (1925). Benchley was a newspaper columnist, magazine writer, and noted humorist. Woollcott was a noted drama critic. And Parker was a humorist, magazine writer, and author of several screenplays, including two nominated for Academy Awards: *A Star Is Born* in 1937 and *Smash-Up: The Story of a Woman* in 1947.

The works by Hemingway, Fitzgerald, and other 1920s authors remain in print today and are often assigned reading in high school and college English classes. Moreover, filmmakers have adapted many of these works into movies. Many of the plays produced during the 1920s have been revived numerous times over the years, often to sold-out theaters.

A Dynamic Era

The era of the Roaring Twenties remains very much alive in American culture. The decade has served as a treasure trove for filmmakers, who have dramatized the gangsters of Prohibition, the flight of Charles Lindbergh, the Algonquin Roundtable, the jazz musicians and athletes of the era, the Scopes trial, and numerous other topics. In 2010 the weekly drama *Boardwalk Empire* debuted on HBO, chronicling the lives of mobsters in Atlantic City, New Jersey, during the era of Prohibition. And in 2011 director Woody Allen released the feature *Midnight in Paris*, a comedy in which a modern-day screenwriter travels back in time to the 1920s, where he meets Hemingway, Stein, Fitzgerald, and other members of the Lost Generation who help him conquer his writer's block.

Nearly a century after the passing of the decade, the Roaring Twenties seem as though they will never go out of fashion. The decade remains a fascinating and dynamic era of American history. It was an era of lawlessness, to be sure, but it was also an era when Americans broke with the ways of the past, learned to have fun, and laid the groundwork for a future in which American science, business, and culture would lead the world.

Source Notes

Introduction: The Defining Characteristics of the Roaring Twenties

1. Quoted in William Thomas Ellis, *Billy Sunday: The Man and His Message*. Philadelphia: John C. Winston, 1917, p. 80.
2. Quoted in Nathan Miller, *New World Coming: The 1920s and the Making of Modern America*. Cambridge, MA: Da Capo, 2003, p. 58.
3. F. Scott Fitzgerald, *The Crack-Up*. New York: New Directions, 2009, p. 87.
4. Ronald Allen Goldberg, *America in the Twenties*. Syracuse, NY: Syracuse University Press, 2003, p. 83.

Chapter One: What Conditions Led to the Roaring Twenties?

5. Quoted in First World War.com, "Henry Cabot Lodge on the League of Nations," August 22, 2009. www.firstworldwar.com.
6. Quoted in Lucy Moore, *Anything Goes: A Biography of the Roaring Twenties*. New York: Overlook, 2011, p. 170.
7. Quoted in Presidential Museums.com, "Warren G. Harding," 2006. http://presidentialmuseums.com.
8. Frances Elizabeth Willard and Anna Adams Gordon, *What Frances E. Willard Said*. New York: Fleming H. Revell, 1905, p. 65.
9. Quoted in Allen Edmonds, "Cass County's Carry Nation Still a Mystery, a Century Later," *Cass County Democrat Missourian*, June 17, 2011. www.demo-mo.com.
10. Mark Edward Lender and James Kirby Martin, *Drinking in America: A History*. New York: Free Press, 1987, p. 143.

11. Quoted in Martin A. Gosch and Richard Hammer, *The Last Testament of Lucky Luciano.* Boston: Little, Brown, 1975, p. 3.

12. Quoted in Gosch and Hammer, *The Last Testament of Lucky Luciano,* p. 43.

13. Emma Goldman, *Living My Life.* Mineola, NY: Dover, 1970, p. 173.

14. Quoted in Miller, *New World Coming,* p. 265.

Chapter Two: The Jazz Age

15. Quoted in Miller, *New World Coming,* p. 313.

16. Earl Hines, "How Gangsters Ran the Band Business," *Ebony,* September 1949, p. 40.

17. Leonard Feather, *The Encyclopedia of Jazz.* New York: De Capo, 1960, p. 25.

18. Quoted in Miller, *New World Coming,* p. 127.

19. Hines, "How Gangsters Ran the Band Business," pp. 43–44.

20. Quoted in Hines, "How Gangsters Ran the Band Business," p. 46.

21. Quoted in Miller, *New World Coming,* p. 309.

22. Quoted in Miller, *New World Coming,* p. 311.

23. Quoted in Miller, *New World Coming,* p. 313.

24. Quoted in Miller, *New World Coming,* p. 314.

25. Quoted in Marilyn Bardsley, "Eliot Ness: The Man Behind the Myth," True TV Crime Laboratory, 2011. www.trutv.com.

Chapter Three: Decade of Achievement and Discovery

26. Quoted in Leonard Mosley, *Lindbergh: A Biography.* Mineola, NY: Dover, 1976, p. 104.

27. Charles Lindbergh, *The Spirit of St. Louis.* New York: Scribner, 2003, p. 197.

28. Quoted in David A. Clary, *Rocket Man: Robert H. Goddard and the Birth of the Space Age.* New York: Hyperion, 2003, p. 121.

29. Quoted in David Halberstam, *The Reckoning.* New York: William Morrow, 1986, p. 67.

30. Quoted in Moore, *Anything Goes,* p. 260.

31. Quoted in Moore, *Anything Goes*, p. 261.

32. Quoted in Moore, *Anything Goes*, p. 263.

33. Quoted in Moore, *Anything Goes*, p. 264.

34. Quoted in Moore, *Anything Goes*, p. 266.

Chapter Four: The Crash

35. Quoted in Lawrence Block, *Gangsters, Killers and Thieves: The Lives and Crimes of Fifty American Villains*. Oxford: Oxford University Press, 2004, p. 59.

36. Emma Goldman, "Was My Life Worth Living?," *Harper's*, May 2000, p. 48.

37. Goldman, "Was My Life Worth Living?," p. 48.

38. Quoted in Jay Robert Nash, *Terrorism in the 20th Century*. New York: Evans, 1998, p. 62.

39. Quoted in Moore, *Anything Goes*, p. 170.

40. Quoted in Miller, *New World Coming*, p. 108.

41. Quoted in David Greenberg, *Calvin Coolidge*. New York: Holt, 2006, p. 10.

42. Quoted in Amity Shlaes, *The Forgotten Man: A New History of the Great Depression*. New York: HarperCollins, 2008, p. 20.

43. Quoted in Edmund Wilson, *The American Earthquake: A Documentary of the Twenties and Thirties*. New York: Farrar, Straus and Giroux, 1979, p. 306.

44. John Kenneth Galbraith, *The Great Crash 1929*. Boston: Mariner, 2009, p. 22.

45. Quoted in Moore, *Anything Goes*, p. 327.

46. Quoted in Donald A. Rapp, *Bubbles, Booms, and Busts: The Rise and Fall of Financial Assets*. New York: Copernicus, 2009, p. 34.

47. Quoted in Stefan Kanfer, *Groucho: The Life and Times of Julius Henry Marx*. New York: Knopf, 2000, p. 126.

48. Quoted in T.H. Watkins, *The Hungry Years: A Narrative of the Great Depression in America*. New York: Holt, 1999, p. 62.

49. Quoted in Watkins, *The Hungry Years*, p. 61.

Chapter Five: What Is the Legacy of the Roaring Twenties?

50. Quoted in Gosch and Hammer, *The Last Testament of Lucky Luciano*, p. 121.

51. Quoted in *Time*, "Corruption in Philadelphia," September 27, 1928. www.time.com.

52. Quoted in Rick Hampson, "Dry America's Not-So-Sober Reality: It's Shrinking Fast," *USA Today*, June 30, 2010. www.usatoday.com.

53. Quoted in Miller, *New World Coming*, p. 379.

54. Andrew Hemingway, "The Tea Party's Ideal Candidate," *Politico*, May 20, 2011. www.politico.com.

Important People of the Roaring Twenties

William Jennings Bryan: He traveled the country pressuring lawmakers to support Prohibition; his efforts paid off when the Volstead Act became law on January 17, 1920. Following that success, he took up the cause against teaching evolution and prosecuted John T. Scopes in 1925 for breaking a Tennessee law that prohibited teaching evolution to students.

Alphonse "Al" Capone: Capone ran the rackets in Chicago, using ruthless tactics against his enemies: On Saint Valentine's Day in 1929, Capone sent gunmen to kill 7 members of a rival mob. Federal law enforcement officers finally caught up to Capone in 1931 and sent him to prison for 7 years.

F. Scott Fitzgerald and Zelda Fitzgerald: Leading figures of the Lost Generation, Scott Fitzgerald is the author of the novel *The Great Gatsby*, which chronicled life in the Jazz Age; Zelda Fitzgerald is regarded as the consummate flapper, the modern woman who believed her future included more than just motherhood.

Warren G. Harding: Elected president in 1920, Harding's administration was wracked by scandal. He was duped by interior secretary Albert Fall into giving away valuable oil leases on public land in Teapot Dome, Wyoming. Dogged by the scandal, Harding fell into a deep depression and died in 1923.

Herbert Hoover: The third president to serve in the 1920s, Hoover pledged that the government would not intervene in people's lives. When the stock market crashed in 1929, Hoover was accused of doing too little to rescue the American economy. He was defeated for reelection in a landslide in 1932.

Langston Hughes: A major voice of the Harlem Renaissance, Hughes was a poet, novelist, and playwright. Hughes and the other African American writers of the era gave voice to blacks suffering under the Jim Crow laws of the southern states, laying the intellectual groundwork for the civil rights movement that would rise in the 1950s and 1960s.

George S. Kaufman: A playwright, Kaufman was a leading voice of the Algonquin Roundtable, the group of satirists and wits who met for lunch each day at the Algonquin Hotel in New York City. Kaufman authored many of the hit Broadway plays of the 1920s and 1930s.

Charles Lindbergh: The aviator was the first to fly nonstop across the Atlantic Ocean; the flight in May 1927 took $33^1/_2$ hours. Lindbergh's flight proved that aviation could be a safe mode of transportation; soon after the crossing, airlines started making passenger flights.

Charlie "Lucky" Luciano: As a young boy, the future New York crime boss immigrated to America. He organized a gang, won a series of turf wars, and by the dawn of the 1920s ran the bootleg trade in the nation's largest city. In 1936 he was convicted of running a prostitution ring. He spent 10 years in prison and then was deported to Italy.

A. Mitchell Palmer: US Attorney General Palmer declared war on anarchists and ordered federal agents to round up suspects. These arrests became known as the Palmer raids. Some 10,000 suspected Reds were rounded up, often in violation of their constitutional rights, and deported to their home countries in Europe.

George Herman "Babe" Ruth Jr.: His accomplishments on the baseball field helped people forget about the 1919 scandal in which gambler Arnold Rothstein is alleged to have bribed players to lose the World Series. Ruth joined the New York Yankees in 1920. In 1927 he hit 60 home runs—a record that would stand for more than 30 years.

Margaret Sanger: Convinced that multiple pregnancies and births took a toll on women's bodies, many times causing their early deaths, Sanger became an advocate for birth control. She opened the first birth control clinic in the nation, which dispensed contraceptives to women, and established the American Birth Control League.

John T. Scopes: The biology teacher from Dayton, Tennessee, was convicted in 1925 of breaking a state law that prohibited the teaching of evolution. He was fined $100, but two years later his conviction was overturned by the Tennessee Supreme Court. The law prohibiting the teaching of evolution in Tennessee would not be repealed until 1967.

For Further Research

Books

Frederick Lewis Allen, *Only Yesterday*. Garsington, Oxfordshire, UK: Benediction Books, 2009.

William Donati, *Lucky Luciano: The Rise and Fall of a Mob Boss*. Jefferson, NC: McFarland, 2010.

Thomas Kessner, *The Flight of the Century: Charles Lindbergh and the Rise of American Aviation*. New York: Oxford University Press, 2010.

Lucy Moore, *Anything Goes: A Biography of the Roaring Twenties*. New York: Overlook, 2011.

Daniel Okrent, *Last Call: The Rise and Fall of Prohibition*. New York: Scribner, 2010.

Selwin Parker, *The Great Crash: How the Stock Market Crash of 1929 Plunged the World into Depression*. London: Piatkus, 2010.

Phillip G. Payne, *Dead Last: The Public Memory of Warren G. Harding's Scandalous Legacy*. Athens: Ohio University Press, 2009.

Kelly Boyer Sagert, *Flappers: A Guide to an American Subculture*. Santa Barbara, CA: Greenwood, 2010.

Moshik Temkin, *The Sacco-Vanzetti Affair: America on Trial*. New Haven, CT: Yale University Press, 2009.

Websites

The Case of Sacco and Vanzetti (www.theatlantic.com/magazine /archive/1927/03/the-case-of-sacco-and-vanzetti/6625). The *Atlantic* magazine has provided a website featuring an overview of the case against the two suspected anarchists. Written by former US Supreme Court justice Felix Frankfurter, the text provides excerpts from the trial transcript.

Charles Lindbergh: An American Aviator (www.charleslindbergh .com). Maintained by the Spirit of St. Louis 2 Project, which is dedicated to preserving the history of Lindbergh's flight, the site includes a biography of the aviator, time line of the flight, schematic drawings of the *Spirit of St. Louis*, and maps Lindbergh consulted as he flew across the Atlantic.

The Crash of 1929 (www.pbs.org/wgbh/americanexperience/films /crash). Companion website to the PBS documentary *The Crash of 1929*, the site provides interviews with Americans who worked on Wall Street as the stock market plummeted in value, as well as photos from the era.

Famous Cases and Criminals: Al Capone (www.fbi.gov/about-us /history/famous-cases/al-capone). Maintained by the Federal Bureau of Investigation, the website provides a biography of Chicago mob boss Alphonse "Al" Capone. The website includes details on how US Treasury agents built a tax evasion case against the mobster, which sent him to jail for seven years.

Roaring Twenties: History in the Key of Jazz (www.pbs.org/jazz/time /time_roaring.htm). A companion website for the PBS series *Jazz* illustrates how jazz became very popular in the 1920s. Visitors to the website can hear an audio interview with jazz critic Gary Giddins, who describes the link between jazz and Prohibition.

Tennessee vs. John Scopes—The "Monkey Trial" (http://law2.umkc .edu/faculty/projects/ftrials/scopes/scopes.htm). Maintained by the University of Missouri–Kansas City School of Law, the website includes images of pages from the textbook Scopes used in class, as well as political cartoons and photographs of the era.

When Freud Came to America (http://chronicle.com/article/Freuds-Visit-to-Clark-U/48424). The website, maintained by the *Chronicle of Higher Education*, examines psychoanalyst Sigmund Freud's 1909 lectures at Clark University in Worcester, Massachusetts. Freud's lectures helped spark the women's rights movement.

Wilson—a Portrait: The League of Nations (www.pbs.org/wgbh/amex/wilson/portrait/wp_league.html). A companion website to the PBS film *Woodrow Wilson*, the site details the president's plans for the League of Nations and his inability to convince an isolationist US Senate to approve American membership in the league.

Index

Note: Boldface page numbers indicate illustrations.

US Coast Guard, 20–21
US Constitution
  Palmer raids and, 53, 54
  Prohibition and, 8, 15, 16–17, 67
  women's right to vote and, 21
US Securities and Exchange
  Commission (SEC, 1934), 71–72

Vanzetti, Bartolomeo, 54–56
Vicious Circle, 76, 78
Volstead, Andrew, 15
Volstead Act (1919), 14, 15
voting, by women, 21

Walker, James J. "Beau James,"
  "Gentleman Jimmy," 33
Wall Street, bombing of, 52–53
Willard, Frances, 15–16
Wilson, Woodrow, 13–14
Wojciechowski, Earl "Hymie Weiss,"
  37
women
  fashions, 10, 11, 27, 28, 36
  flappers, 27, 36
  Gibson Girls, 36

right to vote, 21
sexual liberation, 23–24
in workforce, 21–23, 22
writers, 76, 77, 78
Women's Christian Temperance
  Union (WCTU), 6, 14–16
Woollcott, Alexander, 76, 78
workforce
  assembly line production, 45
  male domination of, 22
  public works programs, 68–69,
    70, 74
  salaries, 21–22
  unemployment during
    Depression, 61, 64, 71
  women in, 21–23, 22
Works Progress Administration
  (WPA), 74
World War I, 6, 13, 40, 59
World War II, 75, 77

Yale, Frank, 36–37
Yankees, 50

Ziegfeld, Florenz, 30

Picture Credits

About the Author

Hal Marcovitz is a former newspaper reporter and columnist who lives in Chalfont, Pennsylvania. He is the author of more than 150 books for young readers.